KT-118-022

Contents

Preface

In this book I have sought to meet the aims of the Key Concepts series. This is to provide an introduction to a key concept in the social sciences; to discuss some of the main literature in this field; and to provide a commentary on important debates within the subject. All this I have sought to do with respect to ethnicity. In addition I have tried to establish a framework for thinking about ethnicity within the context of 'modernity' or 'late capitalist modernity'. This is an attempt to re-situate ethnicity within a much broader sociological canvas.

In the early chapters I argue that an understanding of 'ethnicity' must be set alongside our understanding of race and nation. The meanings of these words are not the same as that of 'ethnic group' but they cover a great deal of the same terrain and it is important to acknowledge this.

In looking at important debates and literature I concentrate in chapters 4 and 5 on the debates surrounding 'primordialism' or the idea of 'primordial identities'; and on the debates about the work of Nathan Glazer and Daniel Patrick Moynihan which set the tone for much of the discussion of ethnicity in the USA. Although many examples are taken from the USA and the UK I have drawn on materials about Malaysia to show how discourses of ethnicity are articulated in different ways in different social contexts.

In the later chapters I look at some aspects of 'late capitalist modernity' and the place of ethnicity within it. This includes global migration, local and global inequalities, the strength of the state, the theme of individualism, and the question of national identity and majority ethnicity. I have tried to cover key areas in ways which will help new readers as well as providing something for more experienced readers.

Acknowledgements

I am very grateful to Rachel Kerr and Louise Knight of Polity Press who have been very helpful at every stage of the preparation of this book. Their support is very much appreciated.

My colleagues at the University of Bristol, Department of Sociology, have given me a great deal of help. Many thanks to Gregor McLennan for his encouragement. Very special thanks go to Tom Osborne and Harriet Bradley who both read the typescript and gave me excellent critical commentary.

From outside Bristol I have received both important comments and encouragement from John Rex; for this I am most grateful. In recent years I have had the pleasure of meeting up again with my dissertation supervisor Edward Tiryakian and this has been another stimulus to my thinking. My email conversations with Michael Banton have also helped me to clarify things and argue them out. I have had a lot of help and encouragement from Stephen May, now at the University of Waikato.

During a period of study in Malaysia I had the most engaging and informative conversations at Universiti Sains Malaysia in Penang, and University of Malaysia at Sarawak; special thanks to Kntayya Mariappan at USM, Michael Leigh and Zawawi Ibrahim at UNIMAS.

To all these people I am most grateful.

And finally, as ever, my love to Jenny, Alex and Lynda.

Steve Fenton

Introduction

For a term which came to be widely used only in the 1970s, 'ethnicity' now plays an important part in the sociological imagination, and in policy and political discourses. It is worth therefore attempting to be clear about it. In the present volume I have tackled this question along two different lines. One is to establish what ethnicity is, and the second is to determine the conditions under which ethnic identification becomes the principal source of action. In pursuing the first task I have looked at the explicit and implicit meanings of the terms 'ethnic', 'ethnicity' and 'ethnic group', and some closely related terms, particularly 'race' and 'nation'. This included an inspection of some principal writers in the field over the twentieth century to the present. In the second task I have set out to outline, sometimes with knowledge and sometimes speculatively, the circumstances under which ethnic identities become an important dimension of action. The first part of the book addresses the questions most valuable to new students of the field; the second part will, I hope, appeal to new and experienced students alike.

With regard to the definition of ethnicity I take the main debate to be whether, for the purposes of sociological theory, the terms 'ethnic group' and 'ethnicity' refer to sociological realities which are substantial, embedded in group life and individual experience; or whether these terms point to some rather more diffuse and ill-defined identities which have fleeting moments of importance, and should be understood as 'socially constructed' rather than profound and 'real'. On this question I take a position (especially in chapter 3) which occupies the middle ground but is nonetheless precise. In theorizing the conditions under which ethnicity becomes sociologically important – even decisive – I conclude that a theory of ethnicity has to be a theory of the contexts under which it is 'activated'. This conclusion is diffused through the book but it can be rehearsed at the beginning as well as recapitulated at the end. I conclude that:

As a general rule it should be understood that there cannot be a theory of ethnicity, nor can 'ethnicity' be regarded as a theory. Rather there can be a theory of modernity, of the modern social world, as the material and cultural context for the expression of ethnic identities. This is to reject all separation of 'ethnicity' or 'racism' or 'national identity' from the social and theoretical mainstream. It is to re-position the interest in ethnicity within the central domain of the sociological imagination – the structuring of the modern world, class formations and class cultures, and the tensions between private lives, cultures, and the cohesion of communal and public life.

Much of the rest of this book will be an exercise in filling out that argument. We can start by addressing the question of the status of the term 'ethnicity'.

The ontological status of the term 'ethnicity'

The very natural supposition of those who read about ethnicity, or class, or anything else, is that the word refers directly to something 'out there'. The student's wish is to find the definition which is the most precise in capturing this 'thing out there'. Social science seeks to provide these definitions, but there is always the risk that those who write about some 'thing' are said to have created it. One text on ethnicity suggests that the best way of thinking about it is as an intellectual construct of the observers (Banks 1996). A book of readings on class (Lee and Turner 1996) throws up a number of contributors wondering whether we have not been mistaken all along in talking about classes. They raise the possibility not just that classes have disappeared but that they were not there in the first place. And a scholarly article on the 'nation' advises that we should stop using the word; 'forget the nation' he writes (Tishkov 2000). These arguments have been pushed too far: it credits intellectuals with too much power if we suppose that they constructed the things they observe.

Of course, to say that something is an 'intellectual construct' is not the same as saying it doesn't exist. Rather it is reminding us, as Banks rightly does, that whilst something is happening – people march under banners, form associations, kill one another, dress up and dance and sing, follow guidance about whom they should marry – the particular term or terms used to describe these things are the observers' elaborations which can take on a life of their own. This is tantamount to warning 'don't get carried away with your analytical constructs' rather than a warning 'there is nothing there, you are making it up'. In any case it would be dispiriting to think that you were writing a book about something which doesn't exist.

So, I ought to make it clear from the outset that I do think there is something 'out there' which corresponds to what observers call ethnicity. At the same time I do not believe that ethnicity is anything more than a broad and loose denoting of an area of interest; it is not, on its own, a theoretical standpoint, nor is it likely that there can be a unitary theory of ethnicity. But there is something of great interest to be observed and situated theoretically within a sociology of modernity. The simplest way to state what this is, would be by saying that ethnicity is about 'descent and culture' and that ethnic groups can be thought of as 'descent and culture communities'. Now that is just a start and it should be taken as that: a starting point and not a definition. A further step or two would be to say that ethnicity refers to the *social construction* of descent and culture, the social mobilization of descent and culture, and the meanings and implications of classification systems built around them. People or peoples do not just possess cultures or share ancestry; *they elaborate these into the idea of a community founded upon these attributes.* Indeed it is entirely possible for people to elaborate an idea of community despite the fact that claims to sharing descent and culture are decidedly questionable. Two books on *national* 'descent and culture communities' have had great impact with their titles of *The Invention of Tradition* and *Imagined Communities* (Hobsbawm and Ranger 1983; B. Anderson 1983). For all that there is a difference between 'imagined' and 'imaginary', these words 'imagined' and 'invention' have loomed large in the study of ethnic groups, nations and nationalism. Nations and ethnic groups are frequently viewed as socially constructed, imagined or invented, and certainly not as merely groups who share descent and culture. So when we start with this phrase 'descent and culture communities' we should recognize the danger of over-concretizing the communities. But the fashion for imaginings, constructions and inventions may have gone too far. Even where these ethnic labels are rather loose categories of diffuse identifications, there are nonetheless real blocs of the population who correspond roughly to these labels. There really are white Americans of European descent; there really are Malaysians of Chinese descent. When it comes to viewing groups as 'real' and viewing them as 'constructed' we want to have our cake and eat it.

An example of groups and names

Even as early as this introduction it is worth illustrating these ideas with good examples; without substance and application our grand concepts are poor – and dull – things. Any number of examples would illustrate both the idea of 'descent and culture communities' and the idea that such 'communities' are both real and constructed. In a report on Sarawak's population – Sarawak is part of Malaysia in the north of the island of Borneo – in 1968, Michael Leigh listed some 25 ethnic groups and 47 sub-groups (Leigh 1975). Leigh nowhere uses the term 'Dayak' to describe a population although many of the references he cites do. Dayak, a Malay word meaning 'up-country', certainly continues to have currency but is a very loose descriptor for peoples living on both sides of the Malaysia–Indonesian borders. When in 2001 local groups in Kalimantan, Indonesia (on the southern and Indonesian side of the border in Borneo) fought and killed to drive out Madurese, people from the Indonesian island of Madura, being in-migrants who had been settled there by the Indonesian government, these local groups were widely referred to, in the international press, as 'Dayaks' or 'Dayak tribesmen'. On the Malaysian side of the border in Sarawak it is common to hear people described as, for example, Iban or Bidayuh – two 'Dayak' groupings – but the broad term Dayak is often used too, and one of the state's political parties is the *Parti Bangsa Dayak Sarawak* – the Dayak People's Party of Sarawak. In what sense, we could ask, are 'Dayaks' really an ethnic group?

To make the same point in the First World we could ask a parallel question – in what sense are 'Irish Americans' truly an ethnic group?

Fixed categories and diffuse identities

How fixed are these ethnic categories and what do they rely upon? In the Sarawak case they could be said to rely on some of the characteristics of the groups themselves – the language and dialect differences, for instance, are actual and important; people of a particular grouping are identified with certain areas 'up country', and there are, for example, more Bidayuh to the south of the capital Kuching and more Iban in the districts north and east of Kuching; and traditionally there are differences of custom in, for example, the style of construction of longhouses. Certainly an individual Iban or Bidayuh will describe herself or himself as such, although intermarriage across these groups is common. In some respects the real boundary is with Malays and the real sustaining of the boundary is through Islam; thus the distinction between Malays and other Sarawak native peoples is between Muslim and non-Muslim – leaving some eight Chinese dialect groups out of the equation for the moment. But some two thirds of one 'native' group – the Melanau – *did* adopt Islam when other 'Dayak' peoples resisted, and this has made the Melanau an important group whose elite political players may in effect identify with Malays, especially when in peninsular Malaysia.

But partly the answer is not in the characteristics of the groups but in the behaviour of political elites. If there are occasions for appealing to all Dayaks then an astute political leader will do so. No single group – say Bidayuh – is really a large enough group on which to build a political career. So politicians may appeal to Dayaks, or to *Bumiputeras* (indigenous 'sons of the soil'), a status which native peoples of Sarawak share with Malays. So if we think of groups as classifications marking one from another there are any number of boundary lines involved: between Iban and Bidayuh, between Malay and non-Malay, between Muslim and non-Muslim, and between 'Bumiputeras' (groups considered to be 'native' to the country which would include Malays *and* Dayaks but not Chinese) and non-Bumiputeras. Just which boundaries are important will depend on social context and sometimes on political or other advantage. Judith Nagata made this point about Malays and non-Malays in a classic study of Penang (Nagata 1974). All this impels us to conclude that 'groups' are both actual and constructed. It is a mistake to argue that there is 'nothing there' – there clearly is. But at the same time it would be a mistake to think that the 'groups' are self-evident population and community sub-sets with a clear line drawn round each one. And it would also be wrong to think that, for all this ethnic complexity, people's lives are governed by something called 'ethnicity'.

Do people act by reference to their ethnic identity?

This book will often demonstrate that ethnic groups are not so concrete and substantial as people may think, whilst insisting that there is something to be observed – this something is to do with the terms 'descent and culture' and the circumstances, often political circumstances, in which communities defined by descent and culture become a reference point for action, and in particular for political action. Ethnicity is a gather-all term to denote these dimensions of descent and culture and how they are mobilized to sustain public definitions of groups and the boundaries between them; it is not, on its own, an explanation of anything. But as well as addressing what 'ethnicity' is and what 'ethnic groups' are, we are bound to address the crucially important questions that follow: how important are ethnic groups thus defined, and in what sense is 'ethnicity' a causal factor in societies and social action? 'How important are ethnic groups' could be asked as 'how important are descent and culture mobilized as markers between groups?' 'How causal is ethnicity' could be asked as 'do these identities and social attachments which we call ethnic play an independent part, even a leading part, in social action? If people assume an ethnic identity, does it in any sense become a real guide to action?'

The answer to both these questions is conditional. To the first we would say that under some circumstances, people take cultural and descent identities very seriously: in some societies these types of group boundaries play a key role in the social order; in other circumstances they are trivial, unimportant and barely surviving. To the second question we would caution against being misled into thinking that, because something called 'ethnic groups' are involved, the action, conflict and social relations are primarily determined or 'driven' by ethnicity. A very straightforward illustration would be the intense conflict which was played out throughout the 1990s in the former Yugoslavia, and persists into the new millennium. This was very commonly described as ethnic conflict with the more or less clear assumption that the differences and dislikes between the groups were the causes of the conflict. This is almost implied in simply using the term 'ethnic conflict'. As Michael Banton has pointed out, the danger with the term 'ethnic conflict' is that we assume that the conflict referred to is primarily 'ethnic' in nature and cause (Banton 2000). Often it is not. In the Yugoslavia of 1990 we would at least have to answer the question as to why these same suspicions and dislikes had not caused conflicts in the preceding forty years on anything like the scale of the 'break-up period'.

Ethnic cleansing or racial segregation?

One of the notable things about the conflicts in Yugoslavia is that the press (in English) always referred to *ethnic* conflict and *ethnic* cleansing. But conflicts in the USA which bear some similarities (without being full-scale civil war) are described as *racial* conflict and *racial* segregation. Is there some special feature which makes American conflict racial and Yugoslavian conflict ethnic? There are of course real differences in the circumstances of America and the former Yugoslavia but there is no obvious reason, in describing these conflicts, why one is ethnic and the other racial. The answer lies in the fact that different countries, regions and contexts have given rise to different discourses to describe 'local' events and history. In the USA a race discourse is very powerful and the word 'races' continues to be used routinely despite the discrediting of all social theory based on ideas of racial difference. This difference of discourse (cf. Fenton 1999) has elsewhere been described as an 'idiom of race' and an 'idiom of ethnicity' (Banton 2000). In my 1999 book I wrote at length about the distinctions between ethnic and race but concluded that these are also greatly overlapping discourses. In this current book I want to take a step further and add a third term: the idea of nation. Race, nation and ethnic group belong together in a family of concepts and bear strong family resemblances. This is not to say that they all 'mean the same thing' although there are undoubtedly many occasions when they are interchangeable. But they do share a common reference to the idea of a people, or 'people of this kind'. Furthermore social attitudes, social groups and cultural meanings which have been described as 'racial', 'national' and 'ethnic' are *not* a series of distantly related or unrelated topics. They 'sit together' in fact, in theory and in everyday discourse.

In particular, in **chapter 1**, we look at the English-language etymologies of race, nation and ethnic group. No amount of peeling back the layers of meaning of these terms reveals a decisive set of markers. Rather there is a core and shared meaning among all three, with each having particular connotations which are not fully shared with the others. In chapter 2 we examine the way in which particular countries develop discourses of ethnicity which are peculiar to the history and circumstances of that country. To show that even an English-language discourse of descent and culture communities can vary within different national traditions, the British and American discourses of race and ethnicity are compared. The case of Malaysia is examined in order to illustrate a non-English-language discourse.

In chapter 3 we shall examine some aspects of the usage, within sociology and anthropology, of the terms 'ethnic' and 'ethnicity', with an inspection of related terms such as 'race' and 'tribe'. The last two gradually but irretrievably lost favour. In the case of both race and tribe, the long-run tendency has been to replace them with 'ethnic'. We begin by looking at the gradual demise of the term 'race' as critiques of its nineteenth-century scientific meaning as an anthropological classification began to mount. We look at the famous essay of Huxley and Haddon wherein they propose the end of the term 'race' and the use of the term 'ethnic groups'. We then turn to some key writings in the history of the use of the term 'ethnic groups': Weber's oft-quoted essay, Lloyd Warner's writing on American ethnic groups, and Nagata's classic discussion of circumstantial ethnicity.

In chapter 4 we look at a number of leading controversies in this field of study of which the principal one – by some distance – is the series of disputes surrounding the word 'primordial'. This is not just an extension of defining what 'ethnicity' is, which we treat in chapters 1 and 2. It goes right to the heart of how we think about ethnicity within sociological theory and how we think about society. The simplest way of thinking about 'primordiality' is to think of 'first order', as the word implies: sentiments, ties and obligations, and an unquestioned sense of identity which are embedded in the individual from an early age and remain as a fixed point of reference. This is contrasted with a view of ethnicity as a matter of circumstance, convenience and calculation – a kind of 'English when it suits me' or 'Serbian when it benefits me'.

On this view ethnic groups are not simply groups of people who share a culture and have a shared ancestry. Rather, ideas of descent and culture are mobilized, used and drawn upon to give force to a sense of community, of 'groupness' and of shared destiny. But if groups are, in some sense, socially 'constructed', we are bound to ask 'who does the construction?' If myths of group belonging are being created, who is doing it? One simple answer would seem to be: the people themselves who belong to the group. Curiously, this is often a misleading if not frankly wrong answer. There are at least three other prime suspects.

One is that the idea of a group is not constructed by 'us' but constructed 'for us by others'. In colonial situations, a powerful settler or ruling group established the names for 'natives' and these created groups came to take on, over a long period, a distinctive and actual character. Wherever we look in the post-colonial world we find groups whose names and formation are a direct consequence of the colonial encounter. Even in relatively 'free' migrations, as in workers and families from Europe to the USA in the nineteenth century, new immigrants were categorized and often despised by those established in the country (Jacobson 2001). Second, the building of a group identity may be not so much the work of all members of a group, as of an elite within it, or of a party and organizational leaders. The third possible answer is that groups are formed as a consequence of *state* actions, power and administrative fiat. Many constitutions of states in the contemporary world contain laws and executive guidelines and regulations which have the function of, if not quite creating groups, giving them a kind of permanence and substance as socio-legal realities. If you pass laws bestowing privileges or rights on indigenous peoples you must have some way of deciding who is indigenous and who is not. If you forbid marriage or sexual relations between 'A's and 'B's you must be able to define the 'A's and the 'B's.

Ethnic categories are frequently put to some political purpose. In **chapter 5** we examine some of the classical sources of the argument that ethnic groups may have an instrumental and political character; Glazer and Moynihan's essay which popularized the term 'ethnicity' is often seen as a key source of the 'instrumental' view of ethnicity. This view advocates understanding ethnic identifications as having an instrumental purpose, a conferring of advantage in a political contest. In the same chapter the anthropologist Barth's view of ethnic groups, as being constituted by the maintenance of 'boundaries' between socially contiguous groups, is also explored.

In **chapter 6** we turn away from the question of the status of the concept of ethnicity and ethnic groups. We turn towards the question of the circumstances in which ethnic identities are mobilized. We begin by looking at the importance of the migration of labouring populations in the 'making of ethnicity'. Former slavery societies depended on workers who were captured and migrated because they were forced to; this violent beginning has marked all subsequent social relations. In societies which were colonized the colonial power often imported workers in semi-free conditions, as the British did for example in Malaysia, Fiji, Trinidad and the countries of East Africa.

Throughout the nineteenth and twentieth centuries the USA has been a great destination for migrating workers and people fleeing persecution. By the end of the twentieth century many countries and regions have become destinations in a great globalization of population movements. So here we look at the effect of migration and social mobility on the sustaining of ethnic identities. In **chapter 7** we look more directly at the global context of economic inequalities both within and across countries. The hardening of the lines of economic inclusion and exclusion, of security and insecurity, produces divisions which frequently *broadly approximate* to ethnically identifiable populations. They thus condition ethnically informed action. Similarly, state regimes differ greatly in the degree to which they can guarantee any measure of physical, legal and economic security to their citizens. Ethnicity in a precarious state takes on meanings scarcely found in more secure states.

In **chapter 8** we take seriously the term 'ethnic majority'. In most discussions the term 'ethnic minority' is familiar. Logically as well as sociologically the term 'ethnic minority' suggests the ethnic majority. In societies such as Britain, which have only recently developed an awareness of themselves as 'multi-ethnic', the ethnic majority is also the 'silent majority' scarcely conscious of itself as 'ethnic' at all. It is not inevitable that this situation should produce tensions and racisms, but very regularly it does. In a diffuse sense of hostility towards change and modernity, minority ethnicities are targeted as unfamiliar and unwanted along with other symptoms of despised modernity. In the final chapter we set out some of the most besetting contradictions of what we term 'late capitalist modernity'. These relate to the economic sphere, especially in the social production of inequality and unsatisfied expectations. They relate to the sphere of the individual and the social or 'communal' in the tension between a wish for security and the onward rush of individualization. And these contradictions relate to the moral sphere in the tension between a 'universalist' regard for the dignity of the individual and the periodic resurgence of 'control' moralities. This is an outline of a sociology of capitalist modernity which evokes some of the principal themes around which ethnic identities and ethnic antagonisms are played out.

1
Ethnos: Descent and Culture Communities

Shared references

Ethnic group, race and nation are three concepts sharing a single centre – or 'core' – with some notable and important differences at the periphery. Common to all is an idea of descent or ancestry and very closely implicated in all three we find ideas about culture. These ideas about culture will typically include myths about the past, beliefs about 'the kind of people we are', and the idea that 'culture' defines a group in that it may be constituted by language, dress and custom. In this sense they may all be described as 'descent and culture communities'. Ethnic group, race and nation are all viewed, by themselves or by observers, as peoples who have or lay claim to shared antecedents. This idea of shared ancestry may not be as precise as the genealogies of extended families – though how can we tell how many imprecisions are concealed in family trees? – but there is nonetheless a repeating theme of 'people coming from the same stock'. In English this word 'stock' is mostly used with reference to animals so in its use with reference to people it has a strong biological sense, a strong sense of genealogy and type. This sense of shared ancestry can certainly be found in dictionary definitions (below from the *Compact Oxford English Dictionary*, 1993) of all three of these terms:

Race: a group of persons (animals or plants) connected by *common descent* or origin; a tribe, **nation**, or people regarded as of common stock. [*my emphasis*]

Nation: an extensive aggregate of persons, so closely associated with each other by *common descent*, language or history as to form a distinct **race** of people, usually organised as a separate political state and occupying a definite territory. [*my emphasis*]

Ethnic: (an adjective) pertaining to nations not Christian; pertaining to **a race or nation**; having common racial, cultural, religious or linguistic characteristics especially designating a racial or other group within a larger system. [*my emphasis*]

Ethnic, the only adjective, refers to the previous two by listing race and nation and 'common racial, cultural, religious or linguistic characteristics'. The definition of nation refers to common descent and a distinct race of people. And that of race refers to common descent and tribe, nation or people. Clearly all three occupy very much the same meaning territory; not precisely the same but so close as to make it impossible to consider them separately.

Much of the sociological literature on these terms has been concerned to distinguish them by means of separation, that is by distinguishing them in such a way that one makes a clean break from the other. It is far better to start by saying that all occupy the same terrain. Having said this, the next step is to show the respects in which, as we move from the core outwards, they diverge. What they all convey is a sense of a people. This is precisely the meaning of the term in which 'ethnic' has its origins: the classical Greek word *ethnos*. The word has preserved this meaning in modern Greek covering the English sense of both nation and ethnic group (Triandafyllidou et al. 1997).

Liddell and Scott's *Greek–English Lexicon* (1897), the authoritative source on classical Greek usages, cites a number of meanings which are shifts in emphasis in different contexts and at different periods of ancient Greek history. They are:

Ethnos: Number of people living together, body of men; particular tribes; of animals, flocks; (after Homer) nation, people; (later) foreign, barbarous nations; non-Athenians, (biblical Greek) non-Jews, Gentiles, class of men, caste, tribe.

The adjectival form *ethnikos* has two principal meanings: national and foreign.

So, the Greek *ethnos* has the meanings which are attached to the modern English usage of 'nation', as well as terms such as 'peoples', especially foreign peoples, or tribes and castes, plus the adjectival national and foreign. For tribe we might now read 'ethnic group'. We could have added race in its pre-nineteenth-century forms when it had similar connotations of nations and peoples, and even classes. It was the rise of biological and anthropological science in the nineteenth century which gave to 'race' its special meaning of grand divisions of humankind.

The word 'ethnic' found its way into English (after a number of early spellings such as 'aethnycke') and appears to have long had the sense of 'foreign' and of being distinguished from Jewish (i.e. Gentile) and distinguished from Jewish *and* Gentile (i.e. heathen). In fact the *Compact Oxford English Dictionary* (1993) states that 'ethnic' derives from the Greek *ethnikos*, 'heathen', citing this heathen sense despite the fact that the Greek adjective also clearly had the more neutral sense 'national'. Once 'ethnic' or equivalent established itself in English, with the first citation from a written work of 1473, it regularly has the meaning of 'heathen and foreign'. The *Oxford Dictionary* then cites a second set of meanings, mostly dating from the nineteenth century when it becomes generalized, losing the special 'heathen' sense. Thus we have this definition: 'ethnic', *pertaining to race, common racial or cultural character*. By 1935 they are citing Huxley and Haddon (of which more later) and their famous argument for the abandonment of the term 'race' and its replacement by 'ethnic'. The *Oxford Dictionary* also cites the term in its combination with (ethnic) minority group and as a *noun* meaning one who is not a Christian or Jew. In both the USA and Britain the noun form 'ethnics' is used to mean something other than majority.

Before leaving the Greek dictionary we should note three other ancient Greek terms which have a meaning approximating to people or 'class' of people. One is *phylon* for which

Liddell and Scott give the meaning 'race, tribe or class', followed by a second meaning 'nation'. *Phylon* too has a meaning as a class within the animal kingdom. *Genos* is defined as 'race, stock or kin' . This term has a closer link to the notion of family, offspring and descent. But it too can mean tribe 'as a sub-division' of *ethnos* and can mean classes in the animal kingdom. All these words – *ethnos, phylon* and *genos* – cover shared meanings of people, tribe, nation and class, with shades of difference between them. The word for people in Greek which moves away from all these three but nonetheless could be translated as 'people' is *demos*. It is, in Liddell and Scott, given a first meaning of district, country, land, but subsequently 'the people, the inhabitants' of a district or land. It has two further meanings. One is its meaning as 'common people' as against aristocracy, the people of 'the country' by contrast with the elite people of the city. The other is 'in a political sense' the 'sovereign people, the free citizens', this being the sense which modern English users know in the word 'democracy'.

Stock, type, people, breed

Four things are of special interest in this examination of one language (Greek), a language which happens also to be the source of a good deal of modern terminology. *First* is that all these terms mean something like 'people' and all except *genos* were used in ways which today might be translated as nation. *Genos*'s meaning as specific descent group and sub-group being less than a nation is fairly clear. However, *genos* and the Latin equivalent *genus* have provided the English 'genus' which has been used in biological sciences to mean 'stock, race, kind'. *Second*, all of them, bar *demos*, could have the meaning of a 'class' of animals or people; in the animal and plant kingdom, modern biology has adopted *phylon* and *genos*, neither of which, in common usage, has given us words meaning anything like people or nation. *Genos*, though, appears in 'genocide', 'the deliberate extermination of an ethnic or national group'. *Third* an idea of cultural difference is conveyed by the way in which these words for people, and particularly *ethnos*, were used to mean *other* peoples, who spoke other languages, lived in different countries, and in a later context, were not Jews, or were neither Jews nor Christians. *Fourth*, the words make distinctions which had significance within the societies and periods from which they emanate. The Greeks in general and the Athenians in particular expressed this strong sense of difference between themselves and other peoples. Later, distinctions of Jew, Gentile or Christian and others became important. And in the word *demos* for people, the distinction between citizens (free) and unfree persons was the important one.

Nation

The word 'nation' came into English via French from the Latin root *natio* which has provided the word for nation in virtually all Romance languages. It too has an original meaning of a 'breed' or 'stock' of people who share a common descent or were regarded as so doing. The fact that it has something to do with descent is betrayed by the word *natio*'s own root in the verb *nasci* 'to be born'. The *Oxford Dictionary* gives references to usages of 'nation' as early as 1300. The idea of common descent and the idea of people of a territory were both present. Its earliest uses were not solely – as some have implied – in the context of student groups (*nationes*) in medieval universities, identified by country of origin (cf. Greenfeld 1992). The Latin *natio* is clearly quite close in meaning to the Greek *ethnos*. It even shares the biblical sense of *ethnos*; the *Oxford Dictionary* cites English usage of 'nations' meaning 'heathen nations' in biblical use as early as 1340.

The first part of the *Oxford Dictionary* section on 'nation' essays a general definition that we cited earlier:

An extensive aggregate of persons, so closely associated with each other by common descent, language or history as to form a distinct race of people, usually organised as a separate political state and occupying a definite territory.

The source goes on to say that early uses showed more of 'the racial idea' and later uses, the political. Early (1300–86) references described Englishmen ('Ingles man') as a nation. And the *Dictionary* cites Fortescue in 1460 referring to the King being compelled to make his armies of 'straungers' such as 'Scottes, Spanyardes . . . and of other nacions'. In a history of Carolina in Colonial America (1709) the writer says that 'two nations of Indians here in Carolina were at war'. But 'nation' has also had the meaning of a class of persons, or even animals. A 1390 cited work refers to lovers, or gentle people, as a nation ('Among the gentil nacion love is an occupacion') and similarly describes schoolboys as a nation in late seventeenth-century usage. An early eighteenth-century usage refers to animals as 'the nations of the field and wood'.

Race

Finally of this trio we come to the word 'race', again a word which appears in most Romance languages and is cited as derived from the French *race* and the earlier French *rasse*, matched by the Italian *razza* and Portuguese *raça* (*Oxford English Dictionary* 1993). Its earliest uses in the sixteenth century have a sense of 'breeding', persons of the same family or bred from the same ancestors and, like many of the other words we have traced, it could be applied to animals as well as humans. In 1600 it was used meaning 'a nation or tribe of people regarded as of common stock' and there are indications that it was used to mean simply a people of a land or even just a class of people, as in 'a race of heroes'. It was not until the late eighteenth and early nineteenth century that it began to acquire the meaning of 'one of the great sub-divisions of mankind'. By the late nineteenth and early twentieth century it had become the key term in a whole science of classifying the divisions of humankind into physically defined races which were also widely believed to be the basis of differences in ability and temperament in a global racial hierarchy (Balibar and Wallerstein 1991; Banton 1987; Fenton 1999). After challenges to this race science in the early part of the twentieth century, by the 1950s the term 'race' was in retreat. The 1986 *Oxford Reference Dictionary* states that the notion of 'race as a rigid classificatory system or system of genetics has largely been abandoned'.

Looked at etymologically and historically the usages of these three terms 'ethnic', 'nation' and 'race' support the suggestion that all three have a great deal of common ground. Contained in their past and present usages are ideas of common descent, a common belief in shared descent, ideas of class or type, and about the people of a place, country, kingdom or other form of state. Closely associated or implicated in these terms – and especially in *ethnos* and ethnic – are notions of cultural character, language, and difference, and foreignness. It is remarkable to consider that race, nation and ethnic group are frequently considered to be quite different topics: race and racism, nation and nationalism, and ethnic groups and ethnicity. One recent publication dealing with 'racism' states that it does not 'deal with "ethnicity", a topic covered by a different volume' (Bulmer and Solomos 2000).

The demise of race

We have referred to the decline of the term 'race' and this is certainly true by contrast with what may be regarded as the high point of racial terminology and race-thinking – somewhere in the last quarter of the nineteenth century and the first quarter of the twentieth. The Nazi regime in Germany, through to the end of the Second World War in 1945, adopted race science as the guide to its genocidal politics, although academic and scientific attacks on race-thinking had already begun. Race-thinking had four main characteristics: *first*, that it was possible to classify the whole of humankind into a relatively small number of races defined primarily by physical and visible difference; *second*, that races so defined shared not just appearance type but also temperament, ability and moral qualities; *third*, that there was something that could be called 'racial inheritance', whereby the physical and moral qualities of the race were preserved through racial descent; and *fourth*, that the races of the world were hierarchically ordered with something referred to as the White race, the Caucasian race or sub-divisions of these (Nordic, Ango-Saxon) being superior to all others.

All four of these 'propositions' are now either rejected or not regarded as having any social scientific value. Although physical characteristics (such as skin colour and eye and hair formation) are clustered in particular populations, the attempt to arrive at final classifications of races has largely been abandoned. This is both because we know that there is significant variation within populations referred to as 'races' and because of the sheer difficulty of determining boundaries between races, not least because of the movement and mingling of populations. It is, however, the second and third propositions that are most roundly rejected – the idea that racial difference 'predicts' social and moral qualities. There never was anything but speculative support for such arguments and anthropology and sociology now adopt the contrary argument – that social and cultural qualities are socially and culturally transmitted. All these first three taken together were components of the fourth proposition, the equally discredited white supremacist line of argument. (Students who wish to follow some of the points raised here should consult Malik 1996; Barzun 1965; Banton 1977; Jacobson 2001.) It is also important to understand that this basic set of propositions about races, and the very idea that racial difference was so important, made other subsidiary propositions possible. Most significantly the belief among 'white' Western populations in the superiority of the Caucasian race was important in supporting two positions: that white peoples had some historic destiny to rule over or even supersede and eliminate lower races, and that race mixing was dangerous.

Beware: culture and ethnicity are not the same

We have referred to 'descent and culture' as common points of reference, but they are not of equal weight. Descent, the belief in common descent, and the importance attached to common descent are unmistakably components of race, nation and ethnicity. Culture is more problematic. Nations and ethnic groups are not, for example, 'culture groups' in the sense that the boundaries of some cultures are co-terminous with the boundaries of the nation or ethnic group. Cultures are both wider and narrower than, for example, nations. This can be seen if we think of culture and religion. We can distinguish analytically between cultures and religions, the first referring to custom and practice often with reference to a particular group, and the second referring to communities of faith. In practice culture and religion are very much bound up with each other, and are implicated in the definition of boundaries around groups. Thus religious cultures such as Islam and Christianity are part of the cultural definition of some nation-states; but they have also a global presence in the shape of Christians or Muslims *beyond* any particular nation-state. But cultures may also be *narrower* than nations in the sense that all societies, or rather nation-states, are not comprehended by a single culture. They are divided and differentiated by class and regional cultures and differences of language and religion. And it is also possible to speak of culture without attaching it to groups defined by descent, as in civilizational culture, youth culture and class culture. The conflation of 'ethnicity and culture' is nicely put by Danielle Conversi:

In the literature on nationalism, the terms ethnic and culture are often confused. . . . By ethnicity we refer to a belief in putative descent. Ethnicity is thus similar to race. Culture is instead an open project. . . . [but] since culture is necessarily based on tradition and continuity, it is often confused with ethnicity. (Conversi 2000, pp. 134–5)

The proper emphasis on descent is certainly confirmed by the etymological discussion above – the theme of *descent and common origin is much more central than culture*. However, whilst Conversi is technically correct, some compromise is needed. The association of 'ethnic' and 'culture' has become very familiar and the claim to share a culture is so commonly a key component of the claim to 'sharedness' alongside common descent. People, or nations, or ethnic groups are saying, in effect, 'We are the people, we come from the same stock, we live(d) in the same place, and our customs and beliefs are these.'

In this volume we shall continue to deal principally with ethnicity but only whilst understanding that the topic cannot be separated from the other two, race and nation. So with a primary focus on ethnicity, we will continue to be drawn towards 'race, racism, nations, nationalism'. We shall also be dealing with these three representations of 'descent and culture' in the *modern* world; in several respects they are very much modern topics. Ethnic group identities or ethnicity have taken on new and important meanings in modern nation-states; 'race' was the popular, political and scientific word for most of the nineteenth century and much of the twentieth, and racism (as the attribution of inherent and unequal qualities to peoples) remains important, however much a classificatory and biological idea of 'race' has lost its force. Nations and nationalism are a product of modernity, and the nineteenth and twentieth centuries' dominance of the 'nation-state' as a political form is the key to this. Anthony Smith, for example in his *The Ethnic Origin of Nations* (1986), has long argued for the pre-modern origins of ethnic groups or nations but he also is very clear about the link between 'nation' and 'ethnicity'; the latter is important because of the importance of the former:

Nationalism extends the scope of ethnic community from purely cultural and social to economic and political spheres; from predominantly private to public sectors. To make any real headway in the *modern* world, ethnic movements must stake their claims in political and economic terms as well as cultural ones, and evolve economic and political programmes. . . . Even dominant ethnic groups must turn a latent, private sense of ethnicity into a public manifest one, if only to ensure the national loyalty of their members against the claims of other groups . . . Nationalism has endowed ethnicity with a wholly new self-consciousness and legitimacy as well as a fighting spirit and political direction. (Smith 1981, pp. 19–20)

This is not to say that 'descent and culture communities' are new or specifically modern, as Smith has brilliantly shown (1986). But the representation of descent and culture communities in this modern and political language of nation, race and ethnicity is new. In the summary below we clarify the exact nature of the shared terrain of the three concepts.

Defining the core and the divergences

Race refers to descent and culture communities with two specific additions:

1 the idea that 'local' groups are instances of abstractly conceived divisions of humankind, and
2 the idea that race makes explicit reference to physical or 'visible' difference as the primary marker of difference and inequality.

Nation refers to descent and culture communities with one specific addition:

The assumption that nations are or should be associated with a state or state-like political form.

Ethnic group refers to descent and culture communities with three specific additions:

1 that the group is a kind of sub-set within a nation-state,
2 that the point of reference of difference is typically culture rather than physical appearance, and
3 often that the group referred to is 'other' (foreign, exotic, minority) to some majority who are presumed not to be 'ethnic'.

Summary

In this chapter we have traced the meanings of race, ethnic (group) and nation, mainly through the etymological history – the record of usages and meanings recorded in dictionaries. We have concluded that the idea of an ancestry group, of a people linked by common descent however loosely that is thought of, is the core idea of all three terms. These terms also have connotations which are peculiar to the individual word – a core of shared meaning and some word associations which are not shared. Only the word 'race', for example, has a strong association of biological difference linked to a universal classificatory system. The meanings of the words have also changed and some new meanings are relatively recently acquired. In the next chapter we turn to a related theme – the fact that the actual import of the words is found to be different in different societies. By import we mean the force of meaning which the term carries, the emphasis and importance contained within the term. In different cultures and contexts, the import of the words varies accordingly. This we examine by looking at discourses of race and ethnicity in the USA, the UK and Malaysia.

2
Discourses of Ethnicity in Three Settings: The USA, the UK and Malaysia

The final part of the opening exercise in understanding ethnicity is to appreciate that it is an English term, as is 'ethnic groups'. Just how ethnicity is discussed is very much contextual; there is thus a discourse of ethnicity in the USA, in Britain, in Malaysia and many other regions and countries. A discussion of the three mentioned will provide an illustration of contextual variation in the discourse of ethnicity. We refer here to a 'discourse of ethnicity' but in truth there are several discourses. In particular there are three milieux within which the terminology of ethnic (and race and nation) is used. These are the scholarly; the political, civic and public; and the popular or 'everyday' discourse. Much of the time we shall be referring to the scholarly discourse, when we discuss the works of particular social scientists; but equally this terminology is used in public administration, such as in the Census, and Census designers will often take advice from academics on these very points (see Lott 1998; Hirschman, Alba and Farley 2000). Reference to the popular discourse is often speculative. Although we can expect that scholarly and public uses influence popular discourse the reverse is also true. In any case the popular discourse is little studied (but see Cashmore 1987; Wetherell and Potter 1992; Billig 1995; Rodriguez and Cordero-Guzman 1992; Hirschman, Alba and Farley 2000; Waters 1990, 1999).

The USA

The American view of races, popular, political and academic, is grounded in slavery. Jordan has traced the way in which the treatment of African ('Negro') servants was, in the latter half of the seventeenth century, distinguished from the treatment of white indentured servants (Jordan 1968). Africans became not servants but slaves *durante viva* (for life) and their offspring were also slaves. Under the independence constitution slaves were accorded lesser status than free men, and for purposes of taxation and population accounting were reckoned as 60 per cent of a person. They were not regarded as citizens nor as capable of becoming citizens, and the equation of 'Negro' African ancestry with social status became almost perfect. In the last three decades of slavery particularly, the institution was fiercely debated; one significant argument in defence of slavery was that 'Negros' were a race apart, were lower in a hierarchy of races and in civilization, and that slavery guaranteed the proper relationship of 'white' and 'Negro' (Fredrickson 1972, 1988).

As one of the most prominent social historians of 'whiteness' has observed, the idea and the practice of whiteness can be traced to the earliest days of the United States, as well as to the prior colonial condition of slavery:

In 1790 Congress enacted that 'all free white persons who, have, or shall migrate into the United States and shall give satisfactory proof, before a magistrate, by oath, that they intend to reside therein, and shall take an oath of allegiance, and shall have resided in the United States for one whole year, shall be entitled to the rights of citizenship'. So natural was the relation of whiteness to citizenship that, in the debate which followed, the racial dimension of the act remained unquestioned. . . . nowhere did the nation's first legislators . . . pause to question the limitation of naturalized citizenship to 'white persons'. (Jacobson 2001, p. 22)

The abolition of slavery and the attempt to found a non-racial citizenship failed when white solidarity, class interests (Camejo 1976) and political manoeuvres (Vann Woodward 1964) combined to create a segregated society in which racial status, and the dominant position of whites, became a permanent feature of the social structure of the USA. White Americans, and especially white Southerners who had been protected from direct labour competition with black Americans by slavery, combined politically to ensure continued protection from competition once black men and women were formally free. The idea and concept of race became the language and discourse within which relations between 'white and black' were understood. The two principal groups were thought of precisely in this way: as white and black, as two races, as fundamentally different, and as in a relationship of superiority and inferiority.

In colonial America captured and enslaved Africans provided the chief answer to an urgent need for a plantation labour force. In the matter of land and labour, both crucial to the success of the colonies, African slaves were property and they were a labour force to be controlled. And native American Indian peoples were occupants of the land and thus a threat to land ownership and expansion. In the early years of the independent USA the formation of militia of 'free and able-bodied whites' was in response to the potential threat from 'Negro' slaves and native peoples. As Jacobson says, 'The very notion of "providing for the common defence" was inherently racial in the context of slaveholding on the one hand and frontier settlement on the other' (Jacobson 2001, p. 25).

Thus from the outset ideas of freedom and human dignity applied to whites; the ideals of the Enlightenment simultaneously identified the 'enlightened' races and the lower peoples. US citizenship and civic participation was founded on a concept of white and black, of white and red, and of enlightened and savage (see Jacobson 2001; Fenton 1999, chapter 2).

Immigration to the USA

The white population of colonial America and the early United States, that is of the seventeenth, eighteenth and early

nineteenth centuries, was largely drawn from Britain and
Ireland. Then the sources of new population became more
diverse. From 1820 to 1920 some 35 million people came
to the United States from almost every corner of Europe.
As Oscar Handlin has written, the failure of agricultural
economies drew millions of European peasants into the
USA:

From the heart of the continent (what is now Germany) came six
million . . . from the North went two million Scandinavians, . . .
from the South went almost five million Italians, . . . from the East
went some eight million others – Poles and Jews, Hungarians,
Bohemians, Slovaks, Ukrainians, Ruthenians, . . . and before the
century was out three million more were on the way from the
Balkans and Asia Minor. (Handlin 1973, p. 36)

Many of these immigrants were, in their turn, viewed as
undesirable, in the light of their lowly economic position and
their concentration in the poorest quarters of the expanding
industrial cities of the United States. They were the labour
force of expanding industrial capitalism. They were also
repeatedly understood within a discourse of racial difference
as Matthew Frye Jacobson (2001) has so comprehensively
demonstrated. Although early settlers had included Irish
and Scottish, and therefore, in the racial lexicon, 'Celts', the
early citizens of the United States came to view themselves
as Anglo-Saxons, and, predominantly, Protestant. The core
of Jacobson's argument is that throughout the nineteenth
century, newcomers – not Anglo-Saxon Protestants – were
racially apprehended as representatives of racial divisions
within Europe: Celts, Teutons, Nordics, Jews and Slavs. They
were viewed both as inferior to Anglo-Saxons and as a threat
to Anglo-Saxon civilization. Gradually, however, the idea of
racial divisions among Europeans gave way to a pan-
European racial identity of whiteness and the racial concept
Caucasian. Before this seemingly neat racial conception was
confirmed there were some notable ambivalent and ambiguous distinctions to be made.
    Italian immigrants to the late nineteenth-century US South,
already in the grip of Jim Crow practices (the name given
to black–white segregation), may not have been quite

regarded as 'black' but they were certainly not unequivocally 'white':

In certain regions of the Jim Crow South Italians occupied a racial middle ground within the otherwise unforgiving, binary caste system of white-over-black. Politically Italians were indeed white enough for naturalization and for the ballot, but socially they represented a problem population at best. (Jacobson 2001, p. 57)

The new Italian immigrants in New Orleans were regarded as having compromised their racial status by their close relationships with blacks which broke Southern codes of racial separateness. They were seen as dark-skinned and 'like Negroes'. According to Jacobson,

It was not just that Italians did not look white to certain social arbiters, but that they did not act white. In New Orleans Italian immigrants were stigmatized in the post-Civil war period because they accepted economic niches (farm labour and small tenancy for instance) marked as 'black' by local custom, and because they lived and worked comfortably with blacks. (p. 57)

Italians were therefore one of several groups over the long period of immigration to the United States who were viewed as somehow 'in-between' in the racial classification. (For fuller accounts see Jacobson's work cited here, and Barret and Roediger 1997.) In the twentieth century, for example, there was the question of classification of peoples of the Indian subcontinent, of whom those from the northern areas of India were frequently light-skinned. They had also been regarded by anthropologists as being 'Caucasians'. As David Hollinger observes,

The American sense of whiteness was not simply an application of the Caucasian of classical race theory. Immigrants from India were undoubtedly Caucasian according to physical anthropologists in the early twentieth century, but the United States Supreme Court ruled in 1923 that south Asian immigrants and their descendants were sufficiently 'non-white' to be ineligible for naturalization as whites. (Hollinger 1995, p. 30)

When in 1975 the Federal Interagency Committee on Education was given the task of adopting standard racial classifications the purpose had shifted to inclusion rather than exclusion. Measurement and counting by race was presumed to make possible programmes for the assistance of groups who had been and were discriminated against. Juanita Lott suggests that Indians were initially classed as Caucasians and in effect as whites, subsequently to be reclassed as 'Asians' partly as a result of pressure from the Association of Indians in America (Lott 1998, p. 40). Asians in general, including Chinese, Japanese and Koreans, came to constitute a complication of the United States' classifications. After the liberalization of immigration laws in 1965 the growth of these populations by immigration and natural increase was considerable. Only one other broad grouping has had a comparable effect in destabilizing the USA's conceptions of race and ethnicity, and that was the population officially referred to as Hispanics.

Changes of the late twentieth century

By the late twentieth and turn of the twenty-first century these population shifts have been quite dramatic. Not only have the demographic features changed with the arrival or increase of new groups, especially from East Asia, Latin America and the Caribbean, but classifications are being challenged in important ways. This is especially so in the academic discourse and in the official discourse of the Census where established categories continue to prove difficult to sustain (Rodriguez 2000). The most important changes are the increase in the proportion of the population defined as Hispanic, the increased size of the Asian population, the emergence of a social movement of white ethnicities, a heightened awareness of multi-ethnic or multi-racial categories, and the importance of ethnic categories for the distribution of state funds and resources (Lott 1998). These changes have not only led to modification of racial categories but have begun to prompt a question of the category 'race' itself.

There have been several key features of the idea of race in America. One is that races have been regarded as naturally occurring *fundamental* divisions of humankind – and thus of American society. These are seen to be permanent and in some sense 'fixed'. In short, races are seen as real divisions of the population. This has as a corollary that relations between the races are viewed as a special kind of relationship – race relations – and usually seen as in some sense problematic. The American discourse of ethnicity began to shift the emphasis.

Ethnicity and changing ideas of race

Publications in the 1970s began to add a new discourse, that of 'ethnicity', to the debates about communities and difference. Indeed this was a discourse within which 'difference' was the primary idea rather than a hierarchy of (two) races in relationships of conflict and mistrust. The book which popularized the term 'ethnicity' (though not the first usage) was *Ethnicity: Theory and Experience*, a collection of essays edited by Glazer and Moynihan (1975). The perspective was comparative and world-wide including examples from Asia, the (then) Soviet Union, India, China and South America. American blacks were discussed as a case of 'neo-ethnicity', part of a perceived revitalization of ethnic identities in the USA by whites and non-whites alike. In other contexts the terminology of *races* was much more common in relation to 'black' and 'white'. The notion of *'ethnic groups'* was frequently applied to differentiation among whites principally along the lines of countries of origin in (white) Europe. Outside of this example in Glazer and Moynihan's oft-cited book, it is rare to see African Americans discussed as a case of ethnicity or ethnic consciousness.

The questioning of US racial and ethnic categories has stemmed to a considerable extent from the increased importance of the Hispanic population. The ambiguities resulting from 'racial' classifications of Hispanics have been noted by many (see Hollinger 1995) but a study by Rodriguez and Cordero-Guzman (1992) went a long way towards drawing out the lessons for the whole concept of race in America.

They acknowledge that the concept of 'races' as conceived through the nineteenth and at least the first half of the twentieth century is discredited. Insofar as 'race' has survived as a scholarly term it is usually conceded that this is because the idea of 'racial difference' persists in popular and political discourses. Races are what are culturally constructed as races in local discourses. One such is the United States' paradigm of 'race as biologically or genetically based' and unchanging. The white race, they continue, 'was defined by the absence of any non-white blood and the Black race was defined by the presence of any Black blood', an asymmetrical definition reflecting the USA's inequalities of power with respect to definitions of 'race'. The important conclusion is the much wider one which they correctly draw:

Popular definitions of 'race' vary from culture to culture [suggesting] the importance of historical events, development or context in determining 'race'. That there are different systems of racial classification in different countries (and sometimes within countries) is quite counter to the usual perception that most White Americans hold of race in the USA. (Rodriguez and Cordero-Guzman 1992, p. 524)

Their evidence is drawn from a study of the racial or cultural identifications of Puerto Ricans in an interview survey. Their study was able to discount any idea that Hispanics did not understand the question or that they simply searched for an intermediate (between white and black) category to describe themselves. They continued to show that they *understood* race as primarily a cultural category, that is to do with their Puerto Rican identity or Hispanic identity. In the authors' words, 'they emphasise the greater validity of ethnic or cultural identity. Culture is race . . .' This definition of race as 'cultural category' is rare in the USA. The authors are suggesting that it stems from a quite different (from the USA) South American framework for understanding difference.

This is quite at odds with the American Census' own advice on census completion:

How Should Hispanics or Latinos Answer the Race Question?
People of Hispanic origin may be of any race and should answer the question on race by marking one or more race categories shown on the questionnaire, including White, Black or African American, American Indian or Alaska Native, Asian, Native Hawaiian or Other Pacific Islander, and Some Other Race. Hispanics are asked to indicate their origin in the question on Hispanic origin, not in the question on race, because in the federal statistical system ethnic origin is considered to be a separate concept from race. (US Bureau of the Census 2000)

In the Rodriguez and Cordero-Guzman study over half of their respondents chose a category 'other', that is other than the substantive ones offered. This compares with only 4 per cent of the US population who chose 'other' (race) in 1990. Thus Rodriguez and Cordero-Guzman conclude that the American conception of 'race and races' is peculiar to American history and politics, and is not the same as a South American or Hispanic concept of race and races as exemplified by the 'refusal' of Hispanic Americans to fit, or fit neatly, into the racial categories offered. In US census population data for 2000, 15.4 million (5.5 per cent) of the total population classed themselves as 'some other race', that is other than the five principal categories. In the non-Hispanic or Latino population only 467,000 chose 'other race', only 0.2 per cent of the total population. Clearly the 'some other race' category attracts a large number of Hispanics. Through the increased numbers of Hispanics in America, a contrasting and incompatible conception of race has run up against an established American classificatory system.

Since the Rodriguez and Cordero-Guzman study the US Census itself has carried out studies of how respondents reply to questions about their origins when they are tested by asking different samples in subtly differing ways, for example in the order of questions. This test, referred to as the 1996 Racial and Ethnic Targeted Test (RAETT), was extensively discussed and analysed in an issue of *Demography* (Hirschman, Alba and Farley 2000). One of their principal conclusions merits repeating in detail:

In spite of this seeming stability [of race measurement in the US Census], the conceptualisation and the meaning of race have undergone a sea change; a new concept, that of ethnicity, has arisen as well . . . ethnicity now is used increasingly as an inclusive term for all groups considered to share common descent . . . In a 1987 decision granting an Iraqi the right to sue under provisions of the Civil Rights Act of 1965, the Supreme Court ruled that ethnic groups could be considered races because of the historical uses of these terms (*St Francis College* v *Al-Khazraji* 1987). The term ethnicity may eventually supplant race but race remains the term officially used in population censuses as well as in popular discourse. (p. 381)

In reviewing, with great clarity, the history of the Census categories they suggest, as have others, that the conceptualization of race not as a *natural* but as a socially constructed set of categories, is gaining ground. The importance of Hispanic as a 'cultural' (and therefore ethnic?) category has upset the older racial order, as has the growing recognition of 'inter-racial marriage'.

Hispanic origin has been conceptualised as an ethnic category independent of a person's racial classification. Administrative actions and popular understandings however, have created a social position for Hispanics almost equivalent to that of one of the major racial categories. (Hirschman et al. 2000, p. 382)

Although the results of this study as reported by Hirschman et al. are quite complex, two broad findings stand out: one is that allowing multi-racial categories does not greatly alter the proportions of the population falling into the main races as defined by the Census; the second is that if Hispanic is included in a race category option, then Hispanics' response to a race question is greatly enhanced. Where combined race/ethnic categories are offered and respondents can choose Hispanic as their sole identity 56 per cent of the targeted Hispanic sample selected Hispanic in this way. By contrast, when the Hispanic targeted sample were asked a race question first (without Hispanic as a category) 25 per cent stated 'other race', other than the ones offered.

The authors' final conclusions are bold. 'Race', they say, has little or no objective basis and is used despite being increasingly anachronistic. American popular understanding has moved away from fixed biological categories as useful social descriptors and replaced them with an idea of social origins.

The inclusion of the Hispanic category in a combined classification (race/ethnic) has the advantage of changing the census question from the concept of 'race' which is almost impossible to define, to one of 'origins'. 'Origins' seems to be closer to the popular under-standing of diversity in American society . . . (Hirschman et al. 2000, p. 391)

Another work which discusses some of the symptoms of the contradictions in the American race system is David Hollinger's *Postethnic America* (1995), sub-titled 'beyond multiculturalism'. Rather than suggest that the American race system is breaking up, he is concerned that there are intellec-tual and political flows in exactly opposite directions. The *intellectual* flow is in the direction of recognizing that the term 'race' is obsolete; but the *practical* (administrative) and politi-cal flow is tending to consolidate the 'recognition' of races in American life. In administrative practice, five racial categories – white, black or African American, Asian, American Indian and Alaska native, Native Hawaiian and other Pacific islander, plus a 'some other race' category – are increasingly deployed not only in the Census but as instruments of public policy. In a small deviation from these categories Hollinger describes the routine nature of the categories:

On application forms and questionnaires, individuals are routinely invited to declare themselves to be one of the following: Euro-American (or sometimes white), Asian American, African Ameri-can, Hispanic (or sometimes Latino) and Indigenous peoples (Native American). (Hollinger 1995, p. 23)

This he calls the 'ethno-racial' pentagon, or the five great 'ethno-racial blocs' which have an uncanny resemblance to the global categories of nineteenth- and early twentieth-century scientific racism – Caucasian, Mongoloid, Negroid, Amerindian – with Hispanic as the outlier. This solidity of the great races in the American imagination is reproduced by the US Census. Hollinger, much more than Hirschman et al. whom we discussed above, believes this view persists in popular thought, despite the recognition of the concept of races as a scientific and historical error:

Although the insight that ethno-racial distinctions are 'socially constructed' is rapidly gaining ground, it is still obliged to struggle against popular, deeply entrenched assumptions that ethno-racial groups are primordial in foundation. (Hollinger 1995, p. 26)

The view that 'races' are socially constructed, so contrary to the conventional American view, is supported by Sharon Lee's review of census practice. In looking at 100 years of census classification (1890–1990) she highlights four key themes (Lee 1993, p. 75):

1 the historical and continuing importance of skin colour, usually dichotomized into white and non-white, in defining and counting racial groups
2 a belief in 'pure' races that is reflected in a preoccupation with categorizing people into a single or 'pure' race
3 the role of the census in creating pan-ethnic racial groups, and
4 the confusing of race and ethnicity in census classifications.

The main finding of Lee's review of census usages over this hundred-year period was that the categories changed a great deal, but in particular that the Census vacillated between offering *few* categories, presumably for simplicity, and *many* categories, presumably for fine-tuned sophistication. This can be summarized from Lee's findings thus:

1890 eight groups listed of which four were variants of black
1900 five groups when the 'varieties of black', e.g. octoroon, were dropped

1910 and 1920 had six classes and in 1930 ten groups were
   listed
1950 the groups shrank to seven and 1960 went back up to
   eleven
1970 went back down again to nine
1980 and 1990 listed fifteen groups although the 1980 census
   acted on a recommendation that the term 'race' was misleading and should be dropped.

The fluctuations betrayed the fact that the Census, and the
communities of scholars and experts whom they consulted,
not only did not know what the 'final' list of 'races' should
be, but also were not sure what a race was. Equally, none of
these difficulties was enough to discourage the Census from
creating the (changing) categories, nor enough to stop calling
them 'races'. The emergence of Hispanic as a category added
to the confusion in the definition of what Hollinger calls
'ethno-races' or 'ethno-racial blocs'. Thus, in Hollinger's
view, despite varying administrative usage, Hispanic has
become a part of the 'ethno-racial pentagon', the five big
groups – white, black, American Indian, Asian and Pacific
islander, and Hispanic – that really shape American practice
and classification.

That it makes sense to call these blocs race equivalents is borne out
by the demand of the National Council of La Raza that the Census
bureau reclassify Hispanics as a race rather than *merely* an ethnic
group for the census to be taken in the year 2000. (Hollinger 1995,
p. 33; my emphasis)

Thus despite the grounding of Hispanic in a 'cultural' category of speaking a Hispanic language, and the constant
reminder that 'Hispanics may be of any race', the National
Council of Hispanics themselves want Hispanics to be – in
America – a race. There must be something good about being
a race – rather than 'merely' an ethnic group, which must be
a less important thing. It is possible that the 'importance' of
belonging to a 'race' is related to the fact that categorical enumeration and the demonstration of category disadvantage are
the basis of the allocation of funds designed to redress historic oppression and dispossession.

If the logical basis for racial classification has come to be seriously questioned and the practice of classification is and has been highly varied, depending on both periodic changes and circumstance, we are bound to ask what the basis of racial classification is and why it persists in more or less the form that it takes in the Census. The answer now appears to be that the disadvantaged groups in the American population have acquired an interest in the Census categories. The Census categories, and the pattern of disadvantage which they demonstrate, are the basis of the allocation of resources, in programmes designed to maximize equality of opportunity, to compensate for historical discriminations and achieve greater equality of outcome. Thus for the first time in American history racial categories have become a basis for inclusion rather than exclusion.

The tone was set by the US Commission on Civil Rights (1973; cited in Lott 1998, p. 34) who argued that 'racial and ethnic data are essential tools with which to combat discrimination and plan and monitor affirmative action to remedy past racial wrongs'. In 1978 the Office of Management and Budget issued Statistical Directive 15 which established the 'ethno-racial pentagon' (see Hollinger 1995) classification and became a standard for the collection of data by many public agencies. Federal agencies were more and more required by legislation to collect and use enumerations of the population along the lines of Directive 15 and 'increasingly state and local governmental agencies, marketing firms, private industry, and the non-profit sectors also used this same classification' (Lott, p. 47).

It is contemporary and historic racism and inequality which justified, and continue to justify, the classificatory system, and not the existence of 'races'. The imperative to collect data on 'races' in the American population persists despite the Office of Management and Budget's own finding that 'There are no clear, unambiguous, objective generally agreed-upon definitions of the terms "race" and "ethnicity".... The categories do not represent objective "truth" but rather are ambiguous social constructs...' (Office of Management and Budget 1995, cited in Lott 1998, p. 65).

But these groupings, ambiguous and 'constructed' as they are, have a real presence in American legislation and public policy instruments. The construction of races in the USA began as an exercise in the creation of a white society, predicated from as early as the seventeenth century on racialized categories. The single most notable feature of the category of a dominant group (e.g. 'white') is that it is undifferentiated. In the USA the category white is the numerical majority and is a single category covering, until relatively recently, up to 90 per cent of the population. In category terms this huge population, diverse in language, country of origin, class position from the super-rich to the abjectly poor, is united by a single feature, its whiteness, that is its membership of something called the white or Caucasian race. The same is true of the United Kingdom where the counting of ethnicity in the census initially created a single ethnic group 'whites' which included 94 per cent of the population. This suggests that whiteness is viewed as unproblematic, either from the point of view of civic status or from the point of view of discrimination and social inclusion. When whites in the USA *are* differentiated by 'culture and descent' they are classified as ethnic groups according to ancestry. Thus whites have got ethnicity, non-whites have got 'race'. To be a 'race' in the contemporary USA (other than the undifferentiated white race) you need to be a 'minority' in the sense of suffering disadvantage and discrimination. This is indicated both by the fact that countering discrimination is stated as the purpose of enumeration, and by the emphasis on discrimination for the purpose of recognition as a 'race'. Thus, given the dominance of a 'race' discourse in the USA, ethnic groups and ethnic differences often have a 'white' connotation. By contrast in Britain, where the public discourse focuses more on ethnicity, the term 'ethnic groups' retains its meaning of minority status and foreign origins; ethnic groups in the UK are not white. Some of the themes discussed in this chapter will be revisited in chapter 5 when we will look more closely at the discourse of ethnicity, and at the work of those sociological observers who have made a case for the retention of a scholarly language of race, distinct from the idea of ethnicity.

Where have all the races gone? The case of the UK

If an inspection of a single country, the United States, reveals multiple contradictions in the uses of race and ethnicity, even more does a brief comparison with other countries. In the United Kingdom, the census did not record 'race' or 'ethnic origin' at all until 1990. The question of a 'non-white' presence became a public issue in the 1960s when anti-immigrant politics emerged subsequent upon immigration into Britain of people from Britain's former colonies in the Caribbean and India. Official documents consistently used the word 'coloured' in attempts to assess the size and characteristics of the non-white population but, until 1991, proxy measures were used. These were typically based on country of origin, country of origin of parents, and country of origin of the Head of Household (see Fenton 1996). By the 1980s the so-called New Commonwealth population had much higher proportions born in the UK and so the use of country of birth as a proxy for ethnic group became unworkable. When in 1990 the UK census did record ethnic group the word 'ethnic' did not appear on the form; rather categories were provided as responses to a question as to which group best described the individual. But in all reporting of the 1990 data this question was reported as 'ethnic group'. The idea that *everybody* belonged to an ethnic group had entered the public consciousness on an official basis for the first time (Banton 2000). Although the terms 'race relations' and 'racism' remain as important parts of the public language of discussion, the word 'race' and certainly the word 'races' in the plural are less part of the public discourse in the UK when compared with the USA. Indeed the US Census recognizes both 'race' and 'ethnicity' as distinctive concepts and both are recorded. The UK Census has a single discourse which is about ethnic groups and, typically, minority ethnic groups. Thus the British Census shares with the USA the idea of classifying 'minorities', but it calls them ethnic.

However, when in the UK 'ethnic group' was recorded in 1990 a system of classification was devised which was clearly predicated on a broad distinction between white and non-white, the first category comprising 94 per cent of the population. Precisely as in the USA, the interest in finer-tuned differentiation is confined to groups perceived as minorities, and as non-whites. In the UK former Commonwealth countries, especially India, Pakistan, parts of Africa and the British Caribbean, are the substantial 'senders' of so-called non-whites alongside others from the Far East such as Hong Kong Chinese and Vietnamese refugees. If the question were about ethnic groups in the American sense, where it is often used to mean ancestry differences in the white population, then other groups would be recorded as 'ethnic groups', such as people with Irish, Polish, Italian, Australian or American backgrounds, and more recently arrived East Europeans would also be recorded. The main changes for the 2001 census were two: the inclusion of an Irish category under the 'white' heading and the inclusion of a mixed origin category. The inclusion of the Irish category was the first break in the monolithic nature of the 'white' grouping, and an acknowledgement that whites might experience discrimination and social disadvantage. That this discrimination was true of the Irish was a large part of the argument for including this category. As in the United States, by the end of the twentieth century, use of the data to counter social disadvantage on ethnic lines had become the principal stated purpose of the collection of ethnically defined data (Fenton 1996). The managers of the US Census have acknowledged that it is impossible to distinguish race and ethnicity, in part because of the increasing importance of the category Hispanic. In the UK the term 'ethnic' has become the dominant one in the official discourse of the population of the UK, but the group names listed in the census are a curious mixture of race (colour) categories and national origin categories, with both the US and UK censuses treating whites usually as a huge undifferentiated category.

This forces us to conclude that there is no final permanent meaning given to the terms 'race' and 'ethnicity'; where both are used – as in the USA – the distinction is not clear. What distinctions are made, in the UK or the USA, are different from each other and do not conform to any single logic of how the distinction should be made. In Britain South Asian

Indians have been described as 'coloured', 'black' and 'Indian' in different contexts, different constituencies, or at different times. The inescapable conclusion is that both the language used (races, ethnic groups) and the actual classifications which are deemed to be important are a consequence of embedded social practice coming from historical circumstances. These categories are contested both by activist members of the groups and by more (or less) neutral academics and intellectuals, staggered at the inconsistency of it all or acting as advocates for 'their' group. In the USA and the UK these disputes surround words like 'ethnic minority' and 'race'. We should look at another situation, that in Malaysia, where English is only one of the languages in which a discourse of race or ethnicity is conducted.

Discourse of races in post-colonial Malaysia

The British colonial period did not simply invent the descent and culture communities that made up the population of the state which is now Malaysia. But British rule had a profound effect on the emergence of ethnic awareness in Malaysia (Hirschman 1987), for three related reasons. The first is that they were responsible for stimulating the migration into Malaysia of large numbers of Chinese and Indians who remained largely in spheres of life and areas of residence which marked them off from the Malays. The second is that British ideas of racial difference took on a public and official form when racial or ethnic categories were used to classify the population in, for example, the matter of the census. Third, the British had a big hand in stimulating Malay consciousness by proposing an independence constitution based on a non-ethnic or 'universalist' citizenship which threatened any idea of Malay special rights. Subsequently they acceded to a constitution which *did* guarantee Malay special rights and thus built a definition of a Malay into the constitution itself.

In an English-language Malaysian discourse the word 'race' is the one most frequently used to denote these large group definitions – Malays, Chinese and Indians. The *New*

Straits Times is published in English (as well as Malay). The reporting of politicians' speeches (which may have been made in Malay or English) about 'racial conflict' almost always uses this terminology, speaking about the need to build 'racial harmony' or fostering a society in which 'races may live side by side in peace and mutual respect'.

New Straits Times 19 April 2001
Chinese seek knowledge earnestly, Malays don't.
'. . . values and cultural practices hindering development must be eradicated. This was to ensure the progress of the various races in the country was balanced . . . different races with different cultures achieve varying degrees of success.'

New Straits Times 17 April 2001
Bumiputera traders must be bold and emulate other races to succeed.

New Straits Times 1 December 2000
BN [Barisan Nasional/National Front] committed to ethnic co-operation despite loss.
'. . . the electorate in Lunas had voted along religious and racial lines . . . there was no place for racial and religious sentiments.'

In the quotations above the terms 'races' and 'racial' are common. But the third headline refers to the commitment of the Barisan Nasional (the National Front, the party alliance in power) to 'ethnic co-operation' which certainly does not appear to convey anything different from 'racial co-operation'. The emphasis on religion stems from the fact that one of the challenges to UMNO (the United Malay National Organization) comes from the Islamic party. This party (PAS or Parti SeIslam ·Malaysia) is seen by UMNO as a serious threat because of its potential to split the Malay vote. In the first story, Malays and Chinese are described as 'races' but it is clearly the perceived cultural difference which is at issue.

The use of the term 'race' in Malaysia stems from English usage in the colonial period but there is no evidence that it has the same resonance as when used in the UK or the USA. Leaving aside the complexity of Malaysian classifications (Hirschman 1987) the three broad groupings, Malay,

Chinese, Indian, are seen primarily as different in two respects: one in political status, with the Malays representing themselves as indigenous and the true heirs of the land, the second in culture, with a boundary between Muslims and non-Muslims being the most important and frequently effectively marking the Malay–Chinese boundary. The Malay word *ras*, meaning race or racial, is not in such common use as a number of other words which convey a sense of 'people' or 'common origin'.

The word *rakyat* means folk or people but with a sense of 'common people' or 'folk'. It also has a secondary sense of nationality or citizenship with *rakyat Malasia* meaning the Malaysian people or nation. *Warga* also means 'family' and 'people'; in the phrase *warga negara* ('people of the state') it means citizens, and with the Malay suffix and prefix makes *kewarganegaraan* to mean citizenship. Probably more commonly used than either of these is the word *kaum* which has an explicit sense of 'lineage group' but has also come to have a much broader sense of 'community' or even plain 'group'. Indicating its precise lineage sense Judith Nagata suggests that Malays may place value on a claim to Arab descent:

Thus some 'Malays' who have been overseas for a number of years have returned with the new titles of Shah or Khan that demonstrate descent from a Middle Eastern lineage or *qu'om*. This is translated into Malay as *kaum* and has a comparable meaning of 'lineage' or a 'people' but with a definite implication of shared descent. (Nagata 1974, p. 98)

There are also looser meanings of *kaum* as community and group, such as in *kaum cina* (the Chinese community) or *kaum wanita* (women's group). The *Hippocrene Standard Dictionary* (Coope 1993) gives similar meanings but also suggests meanings closer to the language of 'race and ethnicity'. Among these are *kaum kaum kecil* (minorities, *kecil* meaning small) and *perkauman* meaning racialism. *Kaum tasan* meaning elite and upper classes shows that *kaum* can refer to classes or social strata without any explicit 'descent' reference.

Also in common usage is the word *orang* meaning people. The *Hippocrene* gives its first meanings as 'a human being; a man or woman; people generally (especially in the sense of other people)'. It may be combined with national or ethnic names to give senses such as *orang Melayu*, a Malay; *orang Cina*, a Chinese person. (A Bidayuh man talking about his family told me his daughter had married *orang Canada*, a Canadian.) Through the colonial period and right up to today *orang puteh* means a white person and at least in the colonial period meant primarily 'British'. *Orang* is also the word which is most used to refer to peoples indigenous to Malaysia who are not Malays and usually not Muslims. Of these the most frequently used is *orang asli* 'native or indigenous people', and this is reproduced in government statements and documents when referring to 'development' programmes and state policy towards native peoples. *Orang asing* means foreigner and *orang bukit* (literally 'hill people') means aboriginal tribesmen. Equally important, in the Malaysian politics of ethnicity, are the phrases *orang pendatang*, immigrants; and *orang bukan-Melayu*, non-Malays. *Keturunan pendatang* means descendants of immigrants, a phrase which will usually mean the non-Malay and non-*orang asli* population. Within the discourse of immigrants we also see *pendatang haram* 'forbidden' or 'illegal immigrants' which in the 1990s and new millennium would often refer to Indonesians, Bangladeshis and Filipinos.

But at least as common as all of these, and most common of all in political discourse, is the word *bangsa* and its derivatives. Again it has a core meaning of 'descent' but Nagata has suggested that it combines meanings of descent and culture:

The term *bangsa* conveys the double ideas of a people sharing both a common origin and a common culture. Etymologically it is derived from the Sanskrit *vamsa*, 'line of descent'. Emically it has a primordial quality, for it implies that the cultural traits are inalienably and inextricably associated with a particular people ... carried by a community whose ultimate unity derives from a single origin. (Nagata 1981, p. 98)

Thus Malays are a '*bangsa*' – *bangsa Melayu* – although within that single *bangsa*, several sub-groupings could be defined, on the basis of territorial origin including regions of what is now Indonesia (see Hirschman 1987). It may be found in combination with *suku* meaning initially 'limb' or 'part', but also 'tribe' as part of a people; hence *sukubangsa* meaning sub-group within a population. And just as we noted for the word *kaum* above, it may be used in combination with group names to indicate an 'ethnic' or 'national' group, hence *bangsa Cina* and *bangsa India* meaning Chinese and Indians. In this sense and context *bangsa* comes close to a UK or US and English-language sense of ethnic group. But importantly it is also used in combination with Malaysia, the term used to describe the whole country, just as 'Malaysian' refers to all people of Malaysia irrespective of 'ethnic' or 'racial' origin. Thus *bangsa Malasia* means the nation or the Malaysian people. Similarly *Bangsa Bangsa Bersatu* ('unified') means United Nations. In derived forms it can take on the meaning of 'national' although there is an English borrowing word 'nasional' which is used in some contexts. *Bahasa kebangsaan* (or *bahasa nasional*) means national language and *lagu kebangsan* means national anthem.

As well as the neutral 'national' it can also take on a meaning of 'nationalist' as in Parti Kebangsaan Melayu or Malay Nationalist Party; and the *Hippocrene Dictionary* gives *gila kebangsaan* as ultra-nationalist, literally 'madly nationalist'. In Malaysia and other post-colonial societies, the word 'communalism' has described (in English) political groupings or sentiments which are rooted in ethno-national groups such as Malays or Chinese; no doubt *kebangsaan* would be one of the words which could translate 'communalist'. We may conclude that *bangsa* has the original meaning of descent and community of common origin but has broadened out to usages which would translate into English *as both 'ethnic' and 'national' depending on the context*. Furthermore the discourse of *bangsa* in Malaysia is predicated both on the wish to secure a sense of identity of all Malaysians – as in *bangsa Malasia* – and on the differences between groups such as *bangsa Cina* and *bangsa Melayu*. These differences, as we said above, are largely arranged along two principles – the principle of indigenousness which Malays claim and which makes Chinese *keturunan pendatang* (descendants of immigrants), and the principle of culture especially in the form of Islam and non-Islamic, and of language differences.

The importance of indigenousness resides in the claim made by Malays to be the people of the region and specifically the territory which is now Malaysia. During the independence negotiations Malay political leaders feared that a 'universalist' citizenship, which ignored the special position of Malays as indigenes, would threaten to submerge their cultural survival and their material position. This was based on their lesser participation in the 'modern' economy than Chinese and Indians and their over-representation among the rural poor. Thus the opposite of indigenousness – *pendatang* and *keturunan pendatang*, immigrants and their descendants – is also an important 'status' since the repetition of the history of migration tends to undermine the non-Malays' claim to equal rights. On the Malaysian peninsula there are a small number of *orang asli* (who are indigenes but neither Malays nor Muslims) but it was the entry into Malaysia of Sarawak and Sabah, in East Malaysia or North Borneo, which propelled further the idea of indigenes who were not Malays. In East Malaysia non-Malay native peoples are more numerous than Malays and most are not Muslims. Since the logic of the recognition of the special rights of Malays was 'indigenousness' then *orang asli* and the East Malaysian native peoples had to be included. This led to the creation of the term *bumiputera*, translatable as 'sons or princes of the soil', that is native peoples comprising Malays, the great majority, and all other *orang asli*.

Nagata (1981) also refers to this 'newer, administratively created ethnic category, the Bumiputera (or) "sons of the soil"'. She sees it as opposed to the 'equally new and administratively coined term *kaum pendatang* – immigrant community, applied to the Chinese and Indians collectively'. She regarded the term *bumiputera* as an 'artificial' administrative creation and she voiced doubt about whether it would ever gain full 'ethnic currency', even disappearing from the (then) most recent government five-year plan (see Nagata 1981, p. 109). By the eighth national plan in 2001 *bumiputera* was very much alive, featuring in most discussions of employment, education and share ownership as indications of share in the nation's wealth and development. *Bumis* and *non-bumis* have entered popular usage, at least in English-language press coverage of the special rights policies and in discussions of comparative group advancement (note one of the press headlines above). The idea that one looks at, say, numbers of students entering higher education and simultaneously compares *bumi* and *non-bumi* entry is well established in Malaysian public discourse.

Ethnicity and nation in their place

By looking at three cases in some detail we can demonstrate that there is not a single discourse of 'race, ethnicity and nation' but a series of such discourses attuned to the historical demands of specific countries, regions and internal social and political dynamics. In the United States (and colonial America) the historic dynamic of race, ethnicity and nation centred for a long time on the equation of African origin and slave status, and the establishment of a society predicated on racial definitions. The early exclusion of virtually all Africans from recognition or participation as American citizens was augmented, much later, by an extension of this white and non-white rule to almost all other non-white peoples who might seek to enter the USA or become naturalized American citizens. For most of its history the view of America as a universalist democracy is simply insupportable. An idea of race has been central to the idea of the American nation from its inception. The formally non-racial period after the Civil War was short-lived (about eleven years) and shallow-rooted. Even after the post Second World War civil rights period 'race' has continued to be an inescapable theme of American private, public and political life. Ethnic categories are now revitalized by the predication of the distribution of public resources on census ethnic or racial enumerations. Hispanics and Asian Americans have disrupted an exclusively black–white discourse although the emergence of the term 'people of colour' could be seen as a means by which something very much like it has come to replace it or sit side by side with it. Furthermore the emergence of Hispanics and of a partly reactive white ethnicity has meant that the meanings of race and ethnicity are in doubt. At the same time there is no relaxation of the importance which race and ethnicity assume in American nationhood.

In the United Kingdom a 'simple' distinction between black and white did not have the same social force as in the United States. Britain's slaves were several thousand miles away. The debates about abolition of slavery gave impetus to ideas of race but it was never a domestic issue in the way that it was in America. In the early (sixteenth century) formation of ideas of the nation in England religious loyalties were more important than any 'ethnic' ideas (Greenfeld 1992). When England united with Wales and, much later, Scotland and Ireland, Britain's identity was again rooted in religion as Protestant and in hostility to France and the French (Colley 1992), who were Catholic. But Britain's position by the mid- and late nineteenth century as the head of a world empire gave force to a view of (white) Britons as natural masters of (non-white) 'less civilized' peoples. When that empire was drawing to its close, and people from the Caribbean and India arrived to work in Britain, the tacit nature of the idea of Britain and the British as white became very much less tacit. The debate about national identity and multi-ethnicity is just as central at the turn of the millennium as it was in the immigration debates of the 1950s, albeit with some important new meanings as we shall see in chapter 8.

However, by the time 'race' became an issue in British politics in the late 1950s the word 'race' itself was already under heavy suspicion as a spurious scientific term. When the UK came to count ethnicity in the 1991 census it reported the enumerations as population by ethnic group. The fourth national survey of ethnic groups in Britain was titled *Ethnic Minorities in Britain* (Modood et al. 1997) whilst its predecessor had been called *Black and White Britain* (C. Brown 1984). Academic writers are inclined to place 'race' in inverted commas and to hedge their bets by writing of 'race and ethnicity', often without specifying why they are using two terms and what the difference between them is intended to be.

Malaysia provided a crucial example because here is a society where 'race' is a public issue but the discourse is in both English and Malay – and no doubt in Malaysia's many other languages too. Having been part of the British empire, Malaysia has had bestowed upon it elements of a British imperial discourse of races and, of course, retains the English language in many areas of life. But Malay is the official language and it, or some variant of it, is spoken by the great majority of Malaysia's people. An inspection of the words used for nation, race and ethnicity in Malaysia betrays many common threads – not least the emphasis on 'descent' – but at the same time clearly confirms that discourses of ethnicity are conformed by local practice and historical priorities. In Malaysia the over-riding concern of the Malay majority was to reduce their fear of being submerged by the wealth, power and success of the Chinese. In the Malaysian case a discourse about indigenes and in-comers and about cultural difference, especially as between Islam and non-Islam, is the principal mode of discussion of both nation and 'race' or ethnic group. For all these concepts, *bangsa* most often supplies the needed word and the ambiguities of its many uses serve to illustrate the ambiguities of the Malaysian ethnic and national problematic rather than inherent ambiguities of the word itself.

Summary: race, ethnicity and context

The meanings which 'race' and 'ethnic group' have had in English-language discourses are context-dependent and certainly change within the same society in response to changing social conditions. In the United States the emergence of new non-white and/or non-English-speaking groups in the population has altered the way that 'racial difference' is conceived. In the United Kingdom in the public discourse the term 'ethnic' is frequently used, especially in official publications, although newspapers and popular discourses sometimes use 'race' and 'ethnic' interchangeably. In Malaysia the concept of ethnic difference primarily surrounds the political question of primacy status for Malays and Malay culture. In chapter 5 we will look more closely at the emergence of ethnicity in the United States, both from those who have advocated this framework and from those who have criticized it.

3
The Demise of Race: The Emergence of 'Ethnic'

The exploration of the word origins, of *ethnos* from Greek and *natio* from Latin, shows that the ideas of ancestry, common origin or descent, and more generally 'peoplehood' are at the core of modern usages of the words 'ethnic' and 'nation' which are derived from these classical sources. The word 'race' too, as chapter 1 showed, shares many of the same meanings and 'common descent' is a core meaning of race just as it is with the other two words. All three may be regarded as having the same core and as departing from each other at the periphery, that is in the particular shades of meaning associated with each one. The three words converge around a single theme, descent and common origin, and diverge in respect of particular traditions of usage. We may look at this as shown in figure 1.

So although race has had a sense very close to nation (Banton 1987), it also acquired a very special sense of the division of humankind in a physical anthropological sense. 'American Negroes' were a historically particular group with a special position in American society; the use of the word 'Negroes' suggests that they were thought of – at least by some people – as a 'local' example of a 'universal' category 'Negroes'. In other words American Negroes were a determinate social group but were also part of a grand abstraction. 'Ethnie' or ethnic group has many of the same meanings as 'race' when it is used of determinate social groups, as

Shared meaning: descent and culture community	*Specific meanings*
Race	Universal abstract classificatory system
Ethnic group	Foreign, minority
Nation	Claim to self-rule or autonomy; citizenship and the state

Figure 1   Shared meanings: specific meanings

shown by the fact that the two words plus their derivatives are so frequently interchangeable. But 'ethnic group' entirely lacks this association of grand abstraction of universal categories.

Ethnic group (ethnie) and nation

'Ethnie' shares much with 'nation' but lacks the sense of self-governing entity; if an ethnic group wishes to rule itself it needs to start calling itself a nation, as French Canadians have demonstrated. The existence of multinational states shows that 'state' and 'nation' are not precisely equated. But where several nations are recognized within a multinational state there is always a presumption of some association with self-rule. There may be claims to more or less limited autonomy, a demand for self-governance organized as a political movement, and a fear among the established authority that such a claim might arise to threaten a state (Ghai 2000). 'Nation' has this special association with statehood and self-rule. But in other respects the distinction between ethnie (or ethnic group) and nation is slender. It is also in principle possible for nations to strip themselves of all but the loosest ethnic meanings, that is to stress the *civic* rather than *ethnic* criteria for membership of a nation; this is an important divergence. To this crucial topic we shall return later.

Part of the answer to the question 'what is ethnicity' or 'what are ethnic groups' is to be found in some of the main shifts in scholarly usage, and these shifts have often implicated all three terms. In this book we do not set out to trace the entire history of the scholarly uses of race, ethnic group and nation, nor even of ethnic group or ethnicity, our main foci of interest. There is an excellent literature on all these topics (see for example: Banton 1987; Banks 1996; Hall 1998; Greenfeld 1992; Gossett 1965). Our aim here is to single out some important themes and turning points. In anthropology and sociology the term 'ethnic groups' (or 'ethnie') has partly but not wholly replaced 'race and races'; in social anthropology 'ethnic groups' came to be used where once 'tribes' would have been used (see especially Banks 1996); and in political science and sociology the attention to ethnicity has been followed by the recent interest in nations and nationalism, especially with respect to the distinction between civic and ethnic nationalism (Brubaker 1996; Greenfeld 1992; D. Brown 2000). This is a distinction which views the idea of nation as primarily 'civic', in which the 'people' are defined as citizens with a legal status rather than as a people who share ancestry and origins. This is contrary to nationalist themes which stress the shared ethnic origins of the people (Fenton and May 2002).

The demise of race

When we speak of the demise of race it is important to understand what is being discarded. There is no dispute that appearance types based on skin colour, hair type, and facial features are in some rough and broad-based way distributed and clustered geographically. Nor is there any dispute that typical appearance may be associated with national groupings – for example, most Swedish nationals are light-skinned. The idea that has been in retreat in academic usage for more than a century is the proposition that there are a quite small number of 'stocks' of the human race who share physical features, are genuinely members of an ancestral 'family' grouping, and, in race theory, are predicted to have common *non-physical* characteristics such as temperament and ability. Five landmarks may be discerned in the demise of this idea. The first is the effect of Darwinian ideas of evolutionary change which, in scholarship and science but not in the popular imagination, put paid to the idea of 'fixed types'. This meaning of fixed type (see Banton 1977, 1987) came later than an older use of 'race' as synonymous with 'nation'; in scholarship and science the Darwinian idea of change was quite contrary to the idea of type. A second is Durkheim's argument that 'races', which he appeared to treat almost as if they were equivalent to nations, was not a meaningful sociological category and could not be the basis of the explanation of social difference (Fenton 1980). The third was the attack on racial determinism – that is, on the idea that racial characters were the basis of social difference and unequal abilities – by social anthropologists like Franz Boas who effectively argued that social difference was explainable by reference to 'the environment' and culture (1982). Fourth came the concerted attack on the use of the word 'race' at all, by Huxley and Haddon (1935), who notably suggested its replacement by the term 'ethnic groups'. Fifth came the post Second World War Unesco-organized group who determined that the idea of races was imprecise and of limited value and laid the groundwork for the conclusion that the 'problem' to be studied was not 'races' but racism (Rex 1973).

Scholarly, popular and political ideas

The fact that scholarly ideas and popular and political ideas may not run in tandem was reflected by the timing of the Huxley and Haddon essay. A calculated demolition of the idea of race, it was published in the mid-1930s coinciding with the ascendant political philosophy of racial difference in Germany and the genocide that accompanied it. Their thesis shows, they claim, 'the relative unimportance of purely biological factors' (p. 8). They attack racial ideas as mistaken science. This mistake gets in the way of humanity's task of acquiring 'scientific control of the forces operative in society' (p. 8). The front pages of the book are adorned with sixteen pictures of 'European men' with an invitation to readers to match them to national names such as British and Austrian. No doubt the intention was that most readers would fail, illustrating the unreliability of the idea of physical types matching national groups.

They accept that what they call 'group sentiment' is a powerful force, citing the evidence of admonitions in the Bible to avoid intergroup suspicions. 'The stranger that dwelleth with you shall be unto you as one born among you and thou shalt love him as thyself' (The Book of Leviticus, cited in Huxley and Haddon, p. 12). Humankind is scarcely able to overcome small-group mentalities, as they argue with notably male terminology: 'Mankind has shown itself to be still unprepared to accept the idea of universal human brotherhood. Tribal, religious and national sentiment has time and again overruled the sentiment for humanity' (p. 14).

Much of their thesis is designed to undermine the idea of truly shared ancestry. They recognize that 'common descent' is the core idea of 'race' but argue that the claim of common descent is barely tenable except in the very loosest sense. 'Physical kinship', they say, 'which is frequently suggested as the basis of group consciousness culminating in so-called "race feeling" must be fictitious' (p. 22). They then cite examples of complex mixing and untraceable and uncertain ancestry as evidence of the folly of the idea of real shared descent. Group sentiment is really based on things quite different from the fiction of 'blood'; it is based on occupations, social institutions, religion and custom. The idea of the 'stock' of a nation is a biological fallacy. And the idea of a characteristic physical type is mocked by reference to the very German leaders who were advocating it:

Our German neighbours have ascribed to themselves a Teutonic type that is fair, long headed, tall and virile. Let us make a composite picture of a typical Teuton . . . Let him be as blond as Hitler, as dolichocephalic as Rosenberg, as tall as Goebbels, as slender as Goering, and as manly as Streicher. (p. 26)

This, of course, was mocking since Hitler was certainly not blond – and the other Nazi leaders did not have the characteristics given to them in this passage.

Huxley and Haddon note the use by Herodotus, the Greek historian, of the word *ethnos* (singular) and *ethnea* (plural) as national, regional and language groupings, including the Hellenic *ethnos* itself. 'Herodotus', they say, 'comes to the sensible conclusion that a group such as the Greeks is marked off from other groups by factors of which kinship is one, but that at least as important are language, religion, culture or tradition' (p. 31).

The more Huxley and Haddon examine the attempts to apply the concept of race the more they conclude that it is hopelessly confused and indeterminate. They conclude that 'We can thus no longer think of common ancestry, a single original stock, as the essential badge of a "race"' (p. 106). This quotation is quite possibly the beginning of a long career of 'race' in inverted commas. There is, they suggest, 'a lamentable confusion between the ideas of race, culture and nation' and 'in the circumstances, it is very desirable that the term race as applied to human groups should be dropped from the vocabulary of science' (p. 107). Thenceforth 'the word race will be deliberately avoided and the term (ethnic) group or people employed for all general purposes' (p. 108).

Huxley and Haddon, whilst rejecting the idea of race, were still very much concerned with the range and occurrence of physical characteristics, which they regard as a series of statistical distributions. Only occasionally do they hint at ethnic groups being definable by social location, language and cultural difference and scarcely mention self-identification or a sense of common identity and destiny. That is to say, what they achieved was a scientific demolition of the concept of race. They suggested that population groupings marked by physical difference, geographical location and social environment might properly be called 'ethnic groups' but they did not move on to elaborate 'ethnicity' in the directions it has since taken. They continued to think in terms of distinguishing concrete definable groups rather than thinking of 'ethnicity' as a quality or dimension of social relations. It was the social anthropologists (such as Franz Boas) and sociologists such as Robert Park in America who began to steer the idea of race away from physically differentiated groups towards definition by social position and culture.

Boas certainly took the idea of physical race seriously and the 1982 collection of his essays from the 1930s is full of discussions of anthropometric measures. But he also entertained the idea that culture and environment were important in shaping 'racial difference', a real departure from others writing at the time. Robert Park retained the idea of *racial temperament* thus suggesting that he took the idea of fixed racial difference seriously as a determinant of behaviour. But he also developed a theory of 'race relations' largely predicated on *social* processes of migration and an ecological model of the city (Park 1950). In their work, Park and Boas either gave new meanings to the idea of 'race' or replaced it with 'ethnic group'. Broadly speaking, from this period – Boas, Park, Huxley and Haddon covered the 1920s and 1930s – up until the 1960s, the terms 'races' and 'ethnic groups' continued to be used, in large measure interchangeably, but with (especially) race and (sometimes) ethnic group continuing to have a sense of physically differentiated groups. But the attacks on the certainty and determinacy of the idea of race had begun, and in the world of science and scholarship the concept continued to be in retreat, never to retain its former eminence in the social and anthropological sciences.

Park's work shows how the concept of race, and in particular the idea of racially inherited attributes, persisted despite his own advances in viewing 'races' in their social and historical situations. Thus he speaks of 'the individual man as the bearer of a double inheritance. As a member of a race he transmits, by interbreeding, a biological inheritance. As a member of society or a social group . . . he transmits by communication a social inheritance. The . . . inheritable character . . . constitutes the racial temperament' (Park and Burgess 1921; see the discussion in Banton 1977, p. 102). The individual is therefore seen as inheriting not just physical features, such as skin colour, but also a 'racial temperament'. As an individual he or she is the bearer of a (racial) group characteristic. On the other hand Park's work also shows a global understanding of social change, colonization, and the social effects of European political and economic expansions, within which 'race relations' are worked out (see Fenton

1981). Competition and conflict between racial groups are to be found at the points where capital expands into frontier areas and where Europeans expand their political domains. If the 'racial temperament' discussion gives Park an older ring, the theme of 'global capitalism' makes him sound a good deal more modern.

Lloyd Warner and American ethnic groups

The 1930s in the United States was a notable period for the production of studies of 'race relations', among them classics such as Dollard's *Caste and Class in a Southern Town* (1937) and Davis et al.'s *Deep South* (1941) (see Banton 1977). Lloyd Warner's argument that the American pattern of racial segregation and subordination could be characterized as a colour-caste system came from this period of study. At the time Warner (with Leo Srole) was leading a study of a New England town, part of which was subsequently published (1945) as *The Social Systems of American Ethnic Groups*. This has a particular interest for our present purposes because it combines an interest in what were seen as two different but closely related items of social research – racial groups and ethnic groups. It is interesting because of the distinction between 'racial' and 'ethnic'. But it also gives us a view of how white 'mainstream' America was perceived; it introduces an analysis of caste and class; and their book makes a prediction of how the American racial and ethnic system would evolve.

It is clear that ethnicity (a word not yet used) is, in Warner's view of things, something that 'foreigners' have rather than mainstream Americans; and foreigners are largely people who migrated in the nineteenth and early twentieth centuries from Europe. Although he acknowledges that 'the so-called "old-American" culture is itself new and ultimately "immigrant"', for the most part Warner speaks of 'old' white Americans as just that – Americans – *without 'ethnic' characteristics*. They are the mainstream which others will eventually join. Although he mainly speaks of ethnic groups as more or less recent immigrants to America from Europe, when he comes to define them he combines what he sees as racial and ethnic characteristics. He speaks of five racial types: Light and Dark Caucasoids, two Mongoloid and Caucasoid mixtures (one largely Caucasoid in appearance, the other largely Mongoloid), and Negroes and Negroid mixtures. He does not call them 'races' and only occasionally uses the phrase 'racial groups'. Rather he sees them as racial characteristics which combine with cultural characteristics, language and religion, to give a greater or lesser ease of acceptance in American society. Three types of groups, he says, are ranked as inferior, 'the ethnic group, the racial group, and the ethno-racial group'. The most likely to be accepted are those with racial and cultural characteristics most like those of 'old Americans', that is white, English-speaking and Protestant. The least likely to be readily accepted into the mainstream are those with racial and cultural characteristics most distant from the mainstream. But since 'American Negroes' are like old Americans in 'culture', being English-speaking and Protestant, to say nothing of length of settlement in America, it is clearly their racial characteristics which are seen as causing their exclusion.

Warner pays a lot of attention to three racial types and his use of the words 'Caucasoid', 'Mongoloid' and 'Negroid' have a solid ring of classical race science – that is of the classificatory and typologizing style of writing about 'races' which was so standard in much of the nineteenth century (Banton 1977). But unlike Park who speaks of racial attraction and the inheritance of racial temperament, Warner sees the significance of racial types as lying not in the physical characteristics, that is in what could have been viewed as 'race itself', but in the social meaning attributed to racial difference:

The racial groups are divergent biologically rather than culturally divergent from the old American white population. These traits have been evaluated as inferior. Such physical attributes as dark skin, the epicanthic fold, or kinky hair become symbols of status. ... The cultural traits of the ethnic group, which have become symbols of inferior status, can be and are changed in time; but the physical traits which have become symbols of inferior status are permanent. *Unless the host society changes its methods of evalua-*

tion these racial groups are doomed to a permanent inferior ranking. (Warner and Srole 1945, p. 285; my emphasis)

In Warner's view the destiny of all white or light-skinned ethnic groups is to join the white American mainstream. This is because the force of American equalitarianism 'which attempts to make all men American and alike' combines with social mobility. This produces class differentiation among ethnic groups and thus undermines their solidarity. The class order, he says, 'dissolves our ethnic groups'. By this he means that if immigrants are, in early years of settlement, concentrated in poorer paid work they will also be in the same neighbourhoods, their children will attend the same schools, and their experience of America will be similar. Social mobility will break up these solidarities and similarities and ethnic group cohesion diminishes.

In Warner's discourse then, ethnic means foreign and, through low evaluation of cultural difference, inferior; 'most ethnics are in lower social levels' he writes, using 'ethnics' as a noun. But this ethnic differentiation will fade, an epoch will have ended and the epoch of race will begin (see Warner and Srole 1945, p. 285). The 'host society' in the quotation above ('unless the host society changes its . . . evaluation') must mean white society; after all, most black Americans would have been there much longer than many European Americans. Warner views the status evaluation of racial traits as being unlikely to change. The racial order rests upon, in a later language, the pervasive effect of white racism. Whites appear to be unlikely to change; the possibility that black Americans may take destiny in their own hands and force change is not considered.

Warner's work not only provides an insight into a mid-twentieth-century American view of race and ethnicity. It is also interesting as a benchmark from which to view subsequent events. Less than ten years after the publication of this work the Supreme Court ended legal justification of racial segregation by renouncing the doctrine of 'separate but equal' in the legal case *Brown* vs *the Board of Education of Kansas*, a case brought to contest the exclusion of a black pupil from an all-white school. The court held that the argument that institutions (e.g. schools) could be separate but equal was not sustainable. Not long after that, the pressure of the civil rights movement was bringing even more fundamental changes.

The scholarly tradition: Max Weber and ethnic groups

If we are to have a review of the term 'ethnic groups' in sociology then we should almost certainly begin with Max Weber, who both had an enormous influence on the growth of the subject and wrote systematically about the definition of 'ethnic'. Weber, writing at the beginning of the twentieth century (he died in 1920), is out of chronological order with the American writers mentioned above, but then his writings were not widely known in English-speaking social science until after the Second World War. Even then it was frequently his analysis of capitalism and bureaucratic organization for which he was best known; only recently have contemporary writers interested in ethnicity taken a look back to Weber. A passage from *Economy and Society* (1978) is the most often cited, appearing as a selection in three recent readers (see Guiberneau and Rex 1997; Hughey 1998; Hutchinson and Smith 1996).

The idea of 'racial differences' as objective, as constituted through heredity, and as capable of systematic study is clearly present in Weber. He writes that 'the degree of objective racial difference can be determined . . . purely physiologically, by establishing whether hybrids reproduce themselves at approximately normal rates' (Weber in Hughey 1998, p. 17). This is a statement which takes racial differences as real and worthy of study in a way that the science of races prescribed. His work is therefore another example of the question of 'race' and 'ethnicity' existing side by side, concerned with much the same kind of questions, but with the presumption that 'race' has something to do with physical difference, and sometimes with heritable characteristics.

However, there can be little doubt that the main trend of Weber's argument is sociological, that is to see ethnicity as a *belief in* common descent and then to examine the origins and the consequences of this belief for individual and collective action. Racial or ethnic identities are frequently portrayed as depending on the social perception of difference, and in most cases within the context of political action. This places Weber's ideas close to the ideas of those who, more than fifty years later, spoke of 'political ethnicity' and the sense of common origin being mobilized for political objectives (cf. for example Cohen 1974). Race, he says, 'creates a group only when it is subjectively perceived as a common trait' and becomes the basis of political action when 'common experience of members of the same race are linked to some antagonism against members of an obviously different group' (Weber in Hughey 1998, p. 17).

Three arguments then dominate much of Weber's discussion in this frequently cited passage. One is that common descent is a key element of ethnic identity but it is the *belief* in common origin, not any objective common ancestry, which is socially persuasive. The second is that differences, both cultural and physical, are the reference points around which group identities are formed. Cultural differences may be especially important if they are readily detectable, such as language, or visible, such as dress and aspects of everyday behaviour. These differences are frequently organized into a system of honour such that ethnic honour and status honour are closely related. His example of the 'poor white' in the American South is one such case. The third is the fact that he several times reiterates the idea of an ethnic group as the basis of political action. In this it is closely tied to the idea of nation whose distinctiveness is its orientation to the 'autonomous polity' (Weber in Hughey 1998, p. 28).

The relationships first of ethnicity to political action and second of ethnicity to status have remained as enduring concerns in the study of ethnic groups or 'ethnicity'. In more recent writing (such as Glazer and Moynihan's work which we discuss below in chapter 5; or in the work of political scientists, for example Brass 1985, 1991) ethnically organized groups are regarded as political actors. That is to say, groups are constituted ethnically outside of politics but enter the political arena in order to lobby for their collective interests or even to stake out claims for autonomy. In Weber the emphasis is rather different. He concedes that ethnic groups may pre-date political organization and may then become loosely represented in the organization of a state. But equally he argues that political groups are formed which *then* attribute to themselves an ethnic character:

> The tribe is clearly delimited when it is a sub-division of a polity which, in fact, often establishes it. . . . When a political community was newly established or reorganised, the population was newly divided. Hence the tribe here is a political artifact, even though it soon adopts the whole symbolism of blood symbolism and particularly a tribal cult. Even today it is not rare that political artifacts develop a sense of affinity akin to that of a blood relationship. Very schematic constructs such as those states of the United States that were made into squares according to their latitude have a strong sense of identity; it is also not rare that families travel from New York to Richmond to make an expected child a 'Virginian'. (Weber in Hughey 1998, p. 26)

This is part of a general tendency for political communities to be seen or to see themselves as having common descent. 'All history', he writes, 'shows how easily political action can give rise to the belief in blood relationship, unless gross differences of anthropological type impede it.' Weber's sociological methodology distinguished three types of action: action guided by rationality, affect and tradition (Weber 1978). This was to distinguish action as based on three different guiding principles: rational calculation; sentiment and feeling; and the wish to follow tradition. In these passages about political communities and the belief in common ethnic origin, there are hints that he is regarding 'ethnically oriented action' as an example of action guided by affect and tradition. In this way the 'ethnicization' of political organization or action could be regarded as an instance of the intrusion of non-rational action into rationally organized spheres. In other words states may be organized on rational-legal principles but are, or come to be, influenced by personal or communal sentiments and loyalties. But he concludes by indicating that the category 'ethnically determined social action' (i.e. action guided by the belief in common origin) is too diffuse to be very helpful. This is because it would fail to distinguish so many different aspects of custom and tradition, including those associated with common language, religion, political action, attraction and repulsion, and sexual relations.

The association of ethnic sentiments with the organization of social honour and status is even more central to Weber's argument.

Next to pronounced differences in the economic way of life, the belief in ethnic affinity has at all times been affected by outward differences in clothes, in the style of housing, food and eating habits, the division of labour between the sexes and between the free and the unfree . . . that is . . . all of what affects the individual's sense of honour and dignity. All those things we shall find later on as objects of specific differences between status groups. The conviction of the excellence of one's own customs and the inferiority of alien ones, a conviction which sustains the sense of ethnic honour, is actually quite analogous to the sense of honour of distinctive status groups. (Weber in Hughey 1998, p. 23)

From this point Weber turns his attention to the concepts of nation and nationality. Common descent, or belief in common descent, is again the central idea:

The concept of 'nationality' shares with that of the 'people' – in the 'ethnic' sense – the vague connotation that whatever is felt to be distinctively common must derive from common descent.

Although Weber is quite sure that the belief in common origin is important in political life, and that ethnic evaluations are analogous to status evaluations, he is not sure whether we should take the concept of ethnic groups or 'ethnically determined action' too seriously. That ambivalence has persisted in social anthropology and sociology ever since.

Anthropology and social anthropology

If sociology gradually emancipated itself from the term 'race' and at the very least adopted a language of 'race' and 'ethnicity' existing side by side, social anthropology adopted the terms 'ethnic group' and 'ethnicity' as a means of escaping some unwanted implications of the term 'tribe'. There is available a recent and very good book on the uses of the term 'ethnicity' in anthropology which makes it quite unnecessary to repeat the exercise here. Students wishing to follow the development of an anthropological construction of ethnicity are very well advised to read Marcus Banks, *Ethnicity: Anthropological Constructions* (1996) as an excellent history and theoretical discussion.

Three of Banks' conclusions should be particularly noted here. The first is that 'ethnic group' came to replace 'tribe' under the influence of the members of the Manchester School. These were a group of anthropologists writing in the 1960s and early 1970s and associated with Max Gluckman and Manchester University (see Banks, p. 25; Cohen 1974; Epstein 1978). They recognized the need to see 'tribal' or ethnic identities and behaviour within the explicit context of white colonial power and of urbanization which disrupted 'traditional' behaviour that had been described as 'tribal'. In this way they departed from a convention of viewing a people or tribe as a unitary or self-contained community. *Tribalism* – the persistence in some form of group identities with rural roots in the new urban context – was a problem for colonial administrators and for a modernizing project. But it could not simply be understood as the non-rational loyalties and adherence to custom which the word 'tribal' had come to express. Thus began the notion of 'political ethnicity', the instrumental uses of ethnic identity which were picked up or discarded according to circumstance (see Banks 1996, pp. 24ff).

The second thing to be noted from Banks is that when the term 'ethnicity' came 'into vogue' and into anthropology in the late 1960s it was acknowledged as a term deriving from North American sociology. The *Oxford English Dictionary* records an American usage (of 'ethnicity' rather than just 'ethnic') as early as 1953, but it was the later (1975) volume edited by Glazer and Moynihan which is most often acknowledged as prompting the eventual widespread use of this term. The third item for which (among other things) Banks is an excellent source is the evolution of the specific term *ethnos*

in Soviet anthropological theory. We will look at some of
the main features of this academic tradition because it is so
instructive about the meaning attributed to ethnic groups in
a different language, academic setting and political regime.
Most of what follows is based on Banks' account.

Soviet ethnos

In the 1970s Soviet anthropologists, led by Yulian Bromley,
began to write about ethnic groups, for which they used
the term *ethnos* borrowed from Greek. As post-Stalinist
Russia and the Soviet Union as a whole moved into a more
liberal period it became possible to discuss ethnic groups (or
ethnos-es) as collectivities surviving from pre-socialist into
socialist society. Earlier any recognition of the 'reality' of
ethnic identities, of peoples defined by language, culture and
a belief in common origin, was suspect. It either ran contrary
to Marxist theory which saw modern socialism as trans-
cending ethnicity, or it smacked of 'national' identities which
threatened Soviet citizenship. It was clear to Bromley and his
colleagues that 'ethnos-es' had nonetheless survived, despite
the fearful examples of the persecution of national minorities. They had to be described and analysed with their claws
removed. The solution was to see them as real groupings with
'stable cultural features, certain distinctive psychological
traits, and consciousness of unity' (Banks 1996, p. 19) which
survived through the stages of social evolution but in a
causally subordinate position in relation to economic change.
Ethnoses lived on, material history marched on. In this way
Soviet anthropologists were able to acknowledge 'ethnic
groups' without damaging the materialist theory of history,
and without advancing 'ethnic identities' as any kind of threat
to the Soviet state.

The Soviet episode illustrates two points which we have
referred to previously. The first is that *'ethnos* theory' was
subject to local (in this case Soviet) anthropological discourses, the most important being the Marxist materialist historical paradigm. The second is that the political framework,
in the Soviet instance the subordination of any 'local' national
or ethnic identity to Soviet citizenship, shaped the way in

which the Soviet academicians were able to address the question at all. To accord with a materialist theory of history the *ethnos* was seen as a real and substantive entity in society and history; any undue emphasis on a people's self-definition and collective consciousness was to give too much ground to subjective factors, or even to give anthropological credence to 'nationalist' (non-Soviet) sentiments.

It is therefore notable that within only a few years of the end of the Soviet empire, another leading academician published a classic study of nations and nationalism in the former Soviet zones. Tishkov by this time was pronouncing *a reversal of the theory of ethnicity and nationalism* (Tishkov 1997). Ethnic identities and national identities are *not* naturally occurring social facts grounded in the existence of substantive ethnoses. Rather they are the identities built, shaped and reshaped out of a variety of historical materials, and meet the needs, political exigencies or opportunities of the time. In short they are 'socially constructed' and in great measure a product of circumstance. Thus although Tishkov is clearly concerned by the flame of post-Soviet nationalism (the subtitle of his book is 'the mind aflame') his account of these nationalisms presents them as instrumental and opportunistic rather than as authentic and organic. Only a short time after this publication another article by Tishkov appeared in a leading Western journal, announcing that it was time to abandon the concept of nation altogether (Tishkov 2000).

Real groups

The Russian *ethnos* example not only illustrates how national and regional political agendas frame the way ethnicity and nation are conceived. This example is also a prompt for considering a question about ethnicity which is raised repeatedly. This is the question of whether 'ethnic groups' can be considered as real, organic and substantive groups. This could be regarded as a philosophical question but that is not what I have in mind; the meanings that can be given to the word 'group' can also be tested against observation and evidence.

So the question of 'are ethnic groups real?' is a *sociological question* and not just an *epistemological* one. As a general rule, the further one goes back in sociological and anthropological writing, the more the 'reality' of ethnic groups is assumed or asserted. The further 'forward' we come the less substantive the idea of ethnicity becomes. The problem here, as I have argued elsewhere (Fenton 1999), is not the word 'ethnic' but the word 'group'. The word 'group' implies some measure of collective organization, although the organization may be only loosely articulated. If we look back to Lloyd Warner's ethnic groups, he clearly saw them as definable, relatively distinct and bounded – they were the immigrants from Europe and their descendants who were culturally different and *sustained some forms of group life*. Among the latter would be greater or lesser control of marriage choices (initially disapproving of exogamy), associations to organize welfare such as insurance and burial societies, residential concentrations which made possible collective action in neighbourhoods, schools and churches, and in some instances associations of political defence (Handlin 1973; Yinger 1994). In Warner's account the 'strength of the ethnic subsystem' is indexed by spatial distribution, economic life and the class system, the family, church, language, and the ethnic associations (Warner and Srole 1945). The stronger each of these is in sustaining ethnic culture and group ties, the more the group survives as a real ethnic community which provides a framework for living for its members.

In a rather later work Morris (1968) also gives a substantive definition: 'An ethnic group is a distinct category of the population in a larger society whose culture is usually different from its own. The members of such a group are, or feel themselves, or are thought to be, bound together by common ties of race or nationality or culture.' But in the same article he suggests that 'groupness' ought not to be taken for granted. We should, he writes,

make the distinction between a social group and a social category. By a group sociologists usually mean an aggregation of people recruited on clear principles, who are bound to one another by formal, institutionalised rules and characteristic, informal behaviour . . . it must be organised for cohesion and persistence; that

is to say, the rights and duties of membership must regulate
internal order and relations with other groups. Members usually
identify themselves with a group and give it a name. (Morris 1968,
p. 168)

All of this suggests what I have been referring to as a 'real
groups' conceptualization of ethnicity. But Morris himself
recognizes that such a portrayal is problematic, or at least
may need to be qualified. 'In practice', he says, 'social groups
vary in the degree to which they are corporate' and may
sometimes be a 'mere category of the population' lacking any
of the attributes of corporate life. Judith Nagata makes a
similar distinction. Summarizing the 'etic' (approximately
speaking, the observer's rather than the participant's view)
view of ethnic groups she writes:

Our etic summary of ethnicity as a distinctive social phenomenon
runs as follows: a category or group with some perception of
shared culture, one or more aspects of which will be used primor-
dially as a charter for membership (and for excluding non-
members). It has the capacity for an institutionally self-supporting
and self-sustaining existence. Consciousness, mobilization, and
formal organization may vary from the diffuse identity of a mere
category to the militant activism of a political movement, and this
will be determined by the external social circumstances. (1981,
p. 96)

Just before this passage she has shown how 'ethnic groups'
should be considered as conceptually different from, say,
kinship groups or gender groups:

The final factor seems to lie in the institutional self-sufficiency and
self-reproducing capacity of the ethnic community. Hence the
common association, on the political level at least, with irredentism,
secession, and threats to national integration. (p. 95)

Here Nagata is following some of the arguments of Clifford
Geertz (indeed she cites his famous work, Geertz 1973) in
suggesting that *because* an ethnic group is capable of a kind
of self-sufficiency it poses a threat to 'national integration'
since it may command the loyalty of its members more than

or 'ahead of' the nation. In referring to institutional self-sufficiency and self-reproducing capacity she is setting quite a high test for qualification as an ethnic group. This would mean that such groups were not only culturally distinctive but also institutionally distinctive by having a range of organizations which met many of the needs of the 'members'. Indeed the very word 'members' suggests something quite substantial about ethnicity or ethnic groups. But since ethnic groups are almost always conceived as sections of a larger population in a nation-state it is rarely if ever the case that such institutional separateness is complete. The same is true when groups straddle state boundaries, as do the Basques of France and Spain. In segregated America, for example, there were two sets of institutions for white and black Americans: schools, churches, areas of residence, universities, hospitals, even cemeteries were divided by fences marking black from white. But in Malaysia (where, incidentally, cemeteries are usually ethnically separate – by choice), which will have been the country in Nagata's mind, the amount of institutional 'self-sufficiency' is a matter of degree, and subject to changes in government policy.

Nagata is recognizing this variable degree of organization in the latter part of the first quotation above: 'consciousness, mobilization and formal organization may vary'. In the next phrase is the suggestion that ethnicity may be 'the diffuse identity of a mere category', a phrase which captures almost the opposite of the 'corporate group' idea. But the sting comes in the seemingly harmless and imprecise tail. She says that this variation in political consciousness and organization will depend on 'external social circumstances'. In other words the level of consciousness and political organization of an ethnic group or category will depend less on internal social and cultural features and more on external political and economic circumstances. This would certainly offer an explanation of why ethnic identities may be socially 'quiet' for long periods of time but burst into action when there is a critical change in circumstances. When this happens, people close to the ethnic conflict reflect on how 'we had always got along perfectly well' with their ethnically different neighbours. This was the case in the eruption of ethnic violence in the collapse of Yugoslavia.

The lesson of this discussion, then, is that we should be alert to the possibility that the phrase 'ethnic groups' may carry different meanings in the word 'groups', the apparently innocuous half of the phrase. The variation extends from groups with a real corporate existence to, in Nagata's phrase, *the diffuse identity of a mere category*. If for example we think of the public recording of ethnic origins, the people who nominate 'Pakistani' in the British Census are just that: all those people who checked 'Pakistani' on a form. In what sense they constitute the Pakistani ethnic group or 'ethnic community', as sometimes described, is a matter for sociological investigation. This distinction between the corporate group and the diffuse identity should remain in mind whenever we are considering ethnicity; it frequently is not.

Summary

In the early twentieth century race-thinking was widespread and the idea that the world's population could be classified into unequal races was very much accepted. It was also the time when theoretical critiques of this form of thinking were initiated. Émile Durkheim and Franz Boas, one a French sociologist, the other a German-born anthropologist, led the way in substituting social and cultural explanations for 'racial' ones. The work of the American sociologist Robert Park led in much the same direction. A book by Huxley and Haddon formally proposed the abolition of the term 'race'.

We also addressed the work of Max Weber, the late nineteenth- and early twentieth-century German sociologist who has been possibly the leading classical figure in the founding of sociology. A long excerpt from his essays has been widely cited in contemporary books of readings. Weber remained largely unenthusiastic about the concept of 'ethnic group' but did suggest that its principal meaning lay in a frequently fictitious claim to common ancestry and in its significance in political organization.

We examined the work of Lloyd Warner, the American anthropologist, who wrote a detailed empirical study of American ethnic groups. He mostly viewed ethnic groups as groups who had immigrated to the United States from European states: hence Polish Americans and Irish Americans. He combined his definition of ethnic groups with an idea of racial difference; physically different – in particular black – populations would remain distinct and disadvantaged as long as the white majority treated blackness as low in status.

We discussed the question of how 'real' or 'substantive' ethnic groups are: whether they should be regarded as vague and loosely defined identities, or as corporate groups or naturally occurring and distinct segments of a population. We referred to Marcus Banks' account of the Soviet concept of *ethnos* to illustrate this discussion. This leads us into the next important question concerning 'ethnicity' or 'ethnic groups' – the long-running primordialism debate.

4
The Primordialism Debate

Primordialism

In his book on ethnicity and nationalism in Russia, Valery Tishkov (1997) was anxious to make clear, right at the beginning of his book, that 'primordialism has been definitively discarded in the West'. The Russian social science tradition had failed to learn, 'being heavily dominated by the primordial approach'. They had failed to recognize that identities are socially constructed by ethnic actors themselves and by states, like the Soviet state. Constructivism is opposed to primordialism since 'For primordialists there exist objective entities with inherent features such as territory, language, recognisable membership, and even a common mentality' (p. 1).

For its own reasons (see chapter 3 above) the Soviet state had treated *ethnoses* as objective entities; a post-Soviet turn towards 'constructivism' is understandable enough. The Soviet state sought to objectivize ethnicities so as to make them acceptable divisions of the population as 'naturally occurring' communities of language and culture. This neither threatened the power of the state – since ethnoses were subordinate to the state – nor interfered with the precepts of materialist social science. In short these groups were real, but not very important. But in a post-Soviet Russia, the idea that ethnoses are real is a dangerous one that threatens the new Russian state by posing divisive ethnic nationalisms. Hence the discovery by liberals of 'constructivism'. This methodology tells us that not only do nationalist doctrines elevate the nation to the highest value, but that they also create the very idea of the ethnos or nation itself. Now the groups are not so 'real', but highly dangerous.

But the problem of primordialism is not so simple nor so easily solved as Tishkov would have us believe. In this chapter we shall see how the idea of primordial groups emerged; but first we must be clear about some potentially different meanings of the primordial and the non-primordial. For it is clear that the concept 'primordial' (and its critics) has brought to the surface more than just a discussion of 'objectivist social science' and 'constructionism'. (This is a debate, to be found through much of the history of sociology, as to how much observers simply give names to social facts which have an objective existence, how much they see the social facts and the categories as construed by 'actors' or people in everyday life, and how much they themselves are devising intellectual constructs.) There is at least one other question lying on or just below the surface, and that is: are ethnic identities the subject of calculation and reflection or are they somehow more defined by sentiment and affect than by rationality and calculation? The difficulties in the 'primordialism' debate are heightened by the elision of two questions:

1   Are groups real (or socially constructed)?
2   Are group attachments affective (guided by sentiment) or instrumental (guided by rational calculation)?

We have already made our answer to the first question clear. The understanding of groups as corporate entities and as natural divisions of the population was in need of substantial revision. It was necessary to make way for the argument that identities are in some measure created, sustained and made relevant in political action by ethnically oriented actors and by the state. But the constructionist language of 'invention' and 'imagination' goes too far; for all the invention and re-invention of identities, there are some social realities – of, for example, religious difference, regional concentration, corporate organization and language – which form a substantive base for the construction – and mobilization of ethnic identities. It may be possible to make and to appeal to sharp lines of ethnic difference, but in the absence of any substantive socio-cultural differences, it is hard to imagine how many potentially ethnic actors will answer the call.

'Emotional attachments'

Throughout the whole history of the discipline of sociology there has been a conceptual opposition between an idea of rationality and calculation and an idea of affect, sentiment and emotion. In, for example, the work of Durkheim there is on the one hand an idea of behaviour motivated by interest and on the other, the power of a sense of attachment to a community or 'society' (Durkheim 1933; Fenton 1984). Rational and affective action were central to Weber's ideal types of 'orientations to action'. A similar dichotomy is evident in the Parsonian distinction between instrumental and expressive values (Parsons 1968; Weber 1978). Now this long-standing analytical distinction makes a new appearance in the debates about what kind of social action, social attachment and identity is comprehended by the term 'ethnic'. In popular discourse there is little doubt that ethnic attachments and identities are seen as belonging to the realm of sentiment and 'belonging' as a psychosocial bond. Ethnic sentiments may be seen as not only non-rational but also as defying rationality – that is, despite the gains to be made by acting in a non-ethnic way, people choose to act ethnically. For example despite their shared interests, workers are seen as being deflected from collective class action by ethnic sentiments. Despite an employer's interest in hiring the most able staff, recruiters discriminate on ethnic grounds.

Although social science in some respects prefers a model of rational action, a discourse of emotion or 'sentiment' is undoubtedly diffused throughout the discipline of sociology. Men, in the popular phrase, 'behave badly' because they are guided by an unreasoned sense of masculinity, and behave even worse when that sense of masculinity is threatened. People respond to political slogans because their status is undermined with a resultant sense of diffuse anger or anxiety. Many examples could be given, enough for us to be sure that a language of emotion and sentiment is an explicit or tacit part of sociological thinking. In the field of ethnicity both models are applied: people are seen to be responding to 'blind' group loyalties, or they are seen to be calculating their individual or collective interest. If behaviour in terms of ethnic attachments could be seen to be serving some individual or collective political or economic ends, then the ethnic action could be reinterpreted as *instrumental*. The instrumental character of ethnic attachment was seen as 'calculating' and therefore incompatible with the idea of an unreasoned and affective tie. The latter was described as 'primordial'. Again the solution to this conceptual problem will turn out to be more complex than a simple shift from 'real/natural and affective' to 'constructed and instrumental'. Before we return to a summative consideration we should examine how the term 'primordial' found its way into the literature.

'Primordial' as a sociological concept

The sociological term 'primordial' has no special connection to the problem of ethnicity. Some commentators have failed to recognize this. It has often been discussed as if the concept 'primordial' were invented or elaborated in order to explicate a dimension of 'ethnicity' (Eller and Coughlan 1993). In other words it has been assumed that the debate has been about the question 'is ethnicity a primordial phenomenon?' rather than a quite different question, 'what does the term primordial mean and what assistance, if any, can it provide in explaining ethnic ties and identities?' The first is not a sensible question, the second is. The concept 'primordial' is mostly concerned with the nature and quality of social obligations, a question of 'what kind of society do we live in?' And the question 'what kind of society?' could be rephrased as 'what is the basis of social cohesion?' This is just about the most persistent and long-standing question in the history of sociology. If we are to understand 'societies' or 'social action' we must understand the way in which people are related to, obligated to and identified with each other. This meaning of 'primordial' as one of many attempts to capture the nature of social ties in different kinds of societies – and not as an attempt to define ethnicity – can be traced to a 1950s article by Edward Shils (Shils 1957).

Edward Shils and primordial, personal, sacred and civil ties

Shils first addresses himself to the problem of moral integration in a modern social order. He begins by arguing that the highest ideals, which would include civic or civil values, 'can be lived up to only partially, fragmentarily, intermittently and only in an approximate way'. This proposition about civic values is a very important argument to which we shall return in chapter 9. Shils probably intends this distinction, between the ideal value system and everyday practice, as a feature of all organized societies. But it is particularly interesting as a feature of societies aspiring to civic status, that is of societies who seek to implement some universalistic values about citizenship and duties to 'the whole' which are expected to 'rise above' the ordinary – hence Shils' reference to the sacred as against the purely routine and mundane. Great occasions, national crises, or important occasions such as elections, remind us of civil and sacred ties. At other times our concerns are much more immediate: 'for the rest of the time, the ultimate values of the society, what is sacred to its members, are suspended amidst the distractions of concrete tasks, which makes the values ambiguous and thus gives freedom for individual innovation, creation and adaptation' (p. 131).

The ideologist (meaning here the advocate of the civic ideals) is affronted by people's attachment to 'their mates, family and wish for improvement' (p. 131) but it is the routines of work, family and leisure which generate the sense of obligation and purpose which are the functioning fundamentals of a society as a 'going concern'. Thus modern society is neither merely a market place in which individuals engage with each other only in limited transactions, nor a replication of the moral uniformity of small communities or so-called 'traditional societies'. It has certain grand moral elements, its supreme values and its civic morality, and on great occasions the sacredness of these moral ideas is re-celebrated. But the moral integrity of modern societies is also realized through a multiplicity of obligations and sentiments at a much 'lower order' of social organization. This in fact is Shils' formulation of the 'problem of integration' posed classically by Émile Durkheim (1893), Ferdinand Tönnies (1963) and others, who were concerned to understand how the modern social order could be free, individualistic, open and contractual without becoming hopelessly impersonal and fragmented. Shils' answer is quite explicit:

As I see it modern society is no lonely crowd, no horde of refugees fleeing from freedom. It is no *Gesellschaft* [a reference to Tönnies' concept of a modern society], soulless, egotistical, loveless, faithless, utterly impersonal and lacking any integrative forces other than interest or coercion. It is held together by an infinity of personal attachments, moral obligations in concrete contexts, professional and creative pride, individual ambition, primordial affinities and a civil sense which is low in many, high in some and moderate in most persons.

From this beginning – which contains the first reference to the word 'primordial' – Shils proceeds to review a series of researches which were relevant to the consideration of the role of small groups in large societies. Time and again, he argues, people's attachment to the immediate group within which they are engaged is the main focus of loyalty. The fact that this was so was particularly striking in the case of military units. Here membership of something bigger – the army in service of the country – may have been thought to provoke a wider and higher loyalty. This was not true of either the American army (p. 138) or the Soviet army. The Soviet army was 'a very powerful organisation which had a great deal of coherence, yet very little of that coherence seemed to come from attachment to ideological or political symbols, or even intense patriotism' (p. 143).

In the context of small groups quite intense feelings of loyalty and obligation are generated. This is particularly so within the family because of the significance which is attached to kin obligations. We are not attached to another family member only as a person ('I do like my Uncle Harold') 'but as a possessor of certain "significant relational" qualities, which could only be described as primordial' ('Uncles are important people about whom you must care'). Shils is dismissing a (then) recent argument by George Homans that kin attachments simply flowed from interaction (Shils, p. 142). Rather, he says that the quality of attachment arises 'because a certain ineffable significance is attributed to the tie of blood'.

The main burden of Shils' argument is that primary and civil ties co-exist in the same social order. The former arise from experience within the small group, as in the loyalties developed in army units, or are part of the definition of the relationship, as in 'primordial' ties of kin. The latter, civil ties, are more abstract and called upon and saluted from time to time but not fervently acted out on a daily basis. All in all, Shils is articulating a basis for understanding modern societies and their 'coherence' or 'integration', the fundamental problem as envisaged by the classical sociological tradition (see Nisbet 1967). His own answer is that modern societies are not hopelessly fragmented and 'soulless'; people are not alarmingly detached from each other and lacking in any kind of bonding ties to others; nor are they obligated to the society as a whole because of adherence to some compelling and sacred-like public moral ethos. Rather they have real ties of a 'first order' type within their networks of kin, they have binding ties and sentiments of loyalty within small groups of, for example, the workplace, area of residence, or leisure. And beyond this they have an intermittent sense of obligation to higher-order values, more abstract symbols, and a broader civic sense of duty. The argument corresponds to some elements of Durkheim's sociology of cohesion in modern societies (Fenton 1984). It is certainly an outline theory of the nature of moral and social attachment within a contemporary social order. A good deal of subsequent sociology has been about a parallel question: under what conditions does this routine array of attachments and occasionally enthusiastic commitment to the civil order break down?

We should note that there are two curiosities, possibly contradictions, in what Shils writes. The first is that the term 'primordial' is used in the article but much of his discussion is more properly described as being about '*primary* groups', a much more general reference to face-to-face groups, with whom we are said to feel some strong sense of attachment (i.e. soldiers die for their mates). This is a significant confusion since primary groups are *acquired* in everyday life as well as being 'given' (i.e. not chosen) as in our families. Primordiality is often portrayed as essentially 'given', not acquired. Second, Shils is arguing that these primary attachments are routine and secular, again rather in contrast to the idea that some group memberships, at least on the primordialist view, have a sacredness about them.

Clifford Geertz and the integrative revolution

A second source of the term 'primordial' can be found in an essay by the anthropologist Clifford Geertz, first published in 1973, in his book *The Interpretation of Cultures*. As I have argued in my earlier book (Fenton 1999) Geertz is mainly concerned, in the relevant chapter 'The Integrative Revolution', with the conditions of social and political stability in 'new states', in the immediately post-colonial era of the 1960s. He argues that, in many of the new states, people's primary attachment is to others who are seen to be of the same 'race', who are kinsmen and women, who speak the same language, or whose sense of collective past and future is based on shared experience of a region, of the same religion, or on a community of culture and custom. These communities of custom, kin ties, religion and region are the basis of people's sense of self. These are the real and immediate communities to which people feel that they belong: 'The multi-ethnic populations of the new states tend to regard the immediate, concrete, and . . . meaningful sorting implicit in such "natural" diversity as the substantial content of their individuality' (p. 258).

Two features of this quotation are especially interesting. The first is that the reference to 'immediate and concrete' social attachments almost exactly mirrors Shils' argument as we have set it out above. The second vitally important feature is the quotation marks around the word *natural*. This may not seem much but it is crucial. It is a direct indication that Geertz is regarding these sources of diversity as something other than organic or biological or unchanging human divisions which command the loyalty of their members in a pre-social way. Rather the quotation marks suggest this: people may think of these divisions as natural, we know that they are culturally and socially moulded, as well as being grounded in place, language and shared historic experience.

In the next passage Geertz's argument diverges significantly from that of Shils. Whilst Shils had argued that these primordial attachments existed *side by side* with intermittent commitment to higher-order values, Geertz appears to argue that the strength of the first *interferes with* the flourishing of the latter. Thus he writes that people in new states may find it difficult and risky to 'subordinate these specific and familiar identifications in favour of a generalised commitment to an overarching and somewhat alien civil order'. As a consequence, he argues, new states are '*abnormally susceptible to serious disaffection based on primordial attachments*' (p. 259, my emphasis).There then follows the passage which has been cited more than any other as the basis for outlining the use of the term 'primordial':

By a primordial attachment is meant one that stems from the 'givens' – or more precisely, *as culture is inevitably involved in such matters, the assumed 'givens' of social existence*: immediate contiguity and kin connection mainly, but beyond them the given-ness that stems from being born into a particular religious community, speaking a particular language . . . and following particular practices. These congruities of blood, speech, custom, and so on *are seen to have* an ineffable, and at times overpowering coerciveness in and of themselves. One is bound to one's kinsman, one's neighbour, one's fellow believer, *ipso facto*; as the result not merely of personal affection, practical necessity, common interest, or incurred obligation, but at least in great part by virtue of some unaccountable absolute import *attributed* to the very tie itself. The general strength of such primordial bonds, and the types of them that are important, differ from person to person, from society to society, and from time to time. (pp. 259–60, my emphasis)

This goes a good deal further than Shils in trying to flesh out what a primordial attachment is: there is a sense of obligation to others which is rather taken for granted, and is not a matter of calculation, nor is it the kind of obligation upon which we reflect very much – it is a kind of given, just there. The sentiments surrounding these ties (social attachments, obligations) are not easily put into words (i.e. they are ineffable) but we certainly feel that these are obligations which we can scarcely escape. This deep sense of obligation is not the same thing as the obligation arising from practical relationships, from 'merely personal' affection, or from the reciprocity of exchanges. It is something we feel bound by because of the kind of obligation that it is – like the more or less unquestioned sense of duty we usually feel towards members of our family.

This immediately preceding paragraph, written in my words, is clearly a paraphrase of the Geertz quotation. The only difference is that the second version omits some of the language flourishes of the former – 'congruities of blood', 'absolute import' and the like. Three central ideas come from this passage, in either version. One is that primordial ties are not reflected upon, they are not for the most part a matter of calculation. Second, they are deeply felt and we feel that the obligations or sense of attachment is of a kind that is not easily renounced or evaded. Both the first and second features are evidenced by the fact that they are not easily put into words. Third, 'primordial' describes a kind of attachment which has an importance attached to the tie itself – the absolute import as Geertz describes it. This third part is exactly what the original Shils article describes as 'significant relational qualities'. Shils is arguing that we regard some relationships as different in kind from others. In Shils' case the model type is the kin relationship. As we observed from Shils before: 'The attachment to another member of one's kinship group is not just a function of interaction . . . it is because a certain ineffable significance is attributed to the tie of blood.'

There are other quite important things to notice from this quotation. The most notable, given the nature of subsequent discussion of 'primordiality', are the phrases wherein Geertz is clearly indicating that this kind of attachment and sentiment flows from social attributions and not from any nonsocial nature of the group. This is signalled in the phrases '*assumed* givens', '*are seen to* have a coerciveness' and 'the import *attributed* to the tie itself'. Each of these phrases is indicating a social and cultural process through which a particular meaning is given to these kinds of relationships. This meaning is not, so to speak, there in the first place, or in the nature of the group. It is there because people learn to regard some kinds of relationships as different in quality from others. Nor is primordiality a fixed and universal quality of certain relationships – just how deeply these ties are felt varies from society to society and 'from time to time'.

Equally important as a feature of the elaboration of the term 'primordial' is the list of examples which Geertz provides of the kinds of circumstances which may give rise to this sense of obligation and attachment. There is, for example, in this passage, *no mention of racial or ethnic group*. Geertz is thinking of the sense of place and family, of the sense of belonging deriving from religious identity, from speaking the same language, and from custom. Geertz has in mind parts of the world where such identities are particularly important, and where groups of this kind live precisely side by side. Throughout much of South East Asia we find peoples with different languages (e.g. Malay, Javanese, dialects of Chinese), with different religious identities (Muslim, Christian, Buddhist) and visibly different in custom such as dress and eating habits (pork-eating Chinese, as against Muslims).

After Geertz

The core of the Shils and Geertz argument was that there could be detected relationships which had a distinctive quality – primordial – marking them off from, say, contractual relationships. Nonetheless much subsequent discussion has proceeded on the false premise that *they were defining ethnicity* rather than elaborating an ideal type of relationship. In addition to this the Geertz view has been misrepresented as conceptualizing 'ethnic ties' as almost pre-social, fixed, biological, purely 'emotional' and unreasoning (Eller and Coughlan 1993). This conceptual mis-

representation of what 'primordial' means – and of its
association with ethnicity – has been the basis of an
enduring debate within the sociological literature about
the distinction between 'primordial' and (variously) 'circumstantialist', 'situational', 'instrumental' or other models
of ethnicity (Scott 1990). There are, of course, two distinctive analytical questions: the first asks what is the nature
of the ethnic tie itself, and the second whether or when the
ethnic tie is important. These have been conflated so that
an 'instrumental' view is seen as non-primordial since it
involves calculation as against affect. These different models
could be defined as follows:

Circumstantial: that ethnic identity is important in some contexts
and not others: the identity is constant but circumstances determine
whether it matters;

Situational: that the actual identity deployed or made relevant
changes according to the social situations of the individual: the situation changes, the relevant identity changes;

Instrumental: that the deployment of the identity can be seen to
serve a material or political end and is calculated thus.

None of these actually runs counter to a primordial view
of the nature of ethnicity. To make this clear we can say
that someone may have an ascribed ethnic identity which is
embedded in their personality and life experience, yet still
perceive the circumstances under which it may be instrumental to deploy it.

Judith Nagata

Reference to these divergent views can be found in the work
of Judith Nagata, writing not long after the original Geertz
and Glazer and Moynihan writings (Nagata 1981). Glazer
and Moynihan themselves had made a distinction between a
primordialist and circumstantial view of ethnicity. But they
did so by producing a caricature of the term 'primordial' as
if it meant permanent divisions of societies which were almost

inevitably a source of separation or conflict (Glazer and Moynihan 1975). Glazer and Moynihan, whom we discuss in detail in the next chapter, then correctly point out that this caricatured view is wrong. Ethnicity, they say, is not about 'divisions of human beings into fixed compartments'.

The result has been that a pre-social view of 'primordial' is then contrasted with a 'circumstantialist' view which sees ethnic ties as depending on changing social circumstances and external forces. In other words, whether people feel their ethnic loyalties to be important depends not on the nature of the attachment itself but on the calculation of whether 'in these circumstances' the ethnic tie is one which may be evoked, used and acted upon. Nagata (1981) puts her finger rather neatly on a reason why critics of a 'primordialist' view are so eager to replace it with a so-called circumstantialist view. 'The primordial viewpoint', she observes, 'leaves some social scientists academically uneasy, for they feel poorly equipped to handle such loyalties and sentiments, which seem to slip dangerously out of the world of tangible interests and groups into a half-world of emotion and unreason' (Nagata 1981, p. 89). By contrast we may think of 'ethnic identity and *particularly ethnic mobilisation*' as 'relatively flexible and amenable to change as dictated by external exigencies'.

The distinction here between ethnic *identity* and ethnic *mobilization* is interesting. In the first instance it is a question of explaining how an identity is formed. Why, for example, do people come to regard the language they speak as some kind of mark of group membership, and furthermore as an attachment which is not easily given up or disregarded? This is a question of how social identities are formed. A second question is under what circumstances these identities become the basis for a social movement, for concerted polit-ical action or for any kind of collective organization which goes beyond the routine daily familiarity of the identity itself. That is to say there is a move from 'I am a Malay speaker, I feel at home speaking Malay' to 'We Malay speakers must stick together, organize, defend what we have got' or 'some-times being a Malay is important, sometimes it isn't'.

Nagata's article itself illustrates how circumstances influ-ence how a person will present his or her self. Someone may be significantly a 'Malay' in one context, where for example, as Nagata suggests, there are many non-Malays in the same region. In other circumstances distinctions *among* Malays may become relevant, as among Malays who identify as such but have their origins in neighbouring Sumatra (an island close to Malaysia, and part of Indonesia). Again, depending on circumstances, people may see their place of origin, their ancestry and aspects of custom and culture as fundamental to their being. In these circumstances, she suggests, people attach a 'primordial' meaning to these attributes; they are seen as fundamental, even biological, certainly grounded in place (of birth) and similar in nature to ties of kinship. When 'cultural attributes' are viewed in this way, they may be regarded, Nagata suggests, as being 'primordialized', thus making it clearer than Geertz does that 'primordiality' is bestowed on a relationship and not simply inherent in it.

Much more recently the debate has tended to descend into a rather futile exercise principally based upon an entirely 'straw man' portrayal of 'primordial' attachments. Eller and Coughlan (1993) set out to show that ethnic ties cannot be regarded as primordial by portraying the 'primordial' as something pre-social, or biological or indefinably grounded in emotion. They comment on Shils without acknowledging that Shils was not writing about ethnic groups and, indeed, never uses the word 'ethnic'. They are particularly concerned at the use of the word 'ineffable', finding that it means 'incapable of being expressed in words' or even in other contexts 'not to be uttered, taboo'. Only one page later they write: 'It is well known that social actors are often unable to explain their feelings and behaviours . . . but sociologists ought not to be satisfied with this layman's view of the world.' It is not, however, clear that Geertz is accepting the layman's view as much as describing the nature of the attachment. At this point Eller and Coughlan concede that the errors may not have been so much those of Shils and Geertz but errors of 'subsequent analysts' who saw 'primordial attachments as ineffable and hence un-analysable for sociologists' (p. 190). Of course there is nothing in either of the earlier writers to suggest that 'primordial' ties were 'un-analysable', rather that they may be associated with the kind of sentiments which are taken for granted, assumed as 'givens' and, by and large, not reflected upon or calculated by actors (rather than observers).

It is not easy to say who these subsequent analysts were in Eller and Coughlan's account since virtually all the further literature which they cite is in support of a 'circumstantialist' view of ethnicity. The exception (which they do cite) is the work of Van Den Berghe who has attempted to ground an understanding of ethnic sentiments in sociobiology, a proposition that individual action in accordance with ethnic membership is a group-level extension of a self-preservation principle (Van Den Berghe 1981). The repeated misunderstanding in Eller and Coughlan is their view that Geertz speaks of 'primordial' (ties, obligations, identities) as 'natural' and 'pre-social' rather than socially grounded (compare here the excellent discussion in Gil-White 1999). They appear to think of 'primordial' as meaning prior to all social experience (p. 196); indeed if that were what was meant they would be right in attacking the idea as profoundly un-sociological. If 'primordial' can only mean 'natural', 'biological', 'pre-social', uninfluenced by culture, then Eller and Coughlan are right. In a contest between natural and social, or between nature and society, for sociologists only 'the social' can win. It is difficult to imagine that as distinguished an anthropologist as Geertz thought of human attributes as pre-social or pre-cultural.

Indeed, this is the main lesson which students of sociology should take from this confused and confusing debate. However much *actors* (in sociology meaning people in everyday life as against *observers*) may think of their attachment to a particular ethnic identity as mystically grounded in 'blood', sociologists and anthropologists are almost bound to think otherwise (cf. Gil-White 1999). They will observe that ethnic identities change, the way in which they are formed is not fixed, and the ends which such identities serve – for example, as rallying points in a struggle – may be manipulated by 'ethnic leaders'. This is simply good sociology – there are no pre-social realities. Thus the emphasis on what has been called 'constructionism' in the sociology of ethnicity is nothing more than the good application of a standard sociological theorem: what is seen to be natural by actors is understood by sociologists as socially construed. No doubt there are many actors who also are not deceived.

On this argument, what are described as 'givens' of human existence are precisely the very basic ties, sentiments and cultural attributes acquired through socialization. As John Rex has put it, 'as a matter of empirical fact, there is a set of social ties which is an inevitable part of the human condition' (1996, p. 189). In this sense 'all of us have ethnicity'. Rex is here tying the idea of ethnicity quite closely to family or, more analytically, to socialization. Ethnicity is thus something we are socialized into. Equally important it is something we can grow out of. In arguing this Rex has put the question in a manner very similar to the way I have posed it in this book:

If all this [about socialization] is conceded there is nothing mysterious about the ties involved. They can be comprehended and described sociologically. What is questionable is the suggestion that these ties bind us together with particular others in an unalterable way for life. We do not in fact remain infants all our lives. We may replace the ties which are given to us in our families of birth by others which we choose. In doing so we may identify with an increasingly wide range of chosen others, ties with whom may supplement and may displace those with our immediate community of birth . . . what has to be explained is the extension of the feeling of original ethnic bondedness to a wider range of persons and into adult life . . . the task of the sociologist should be to describe and explain the process by which it happens. (Rex 1996, p. 189)

At least *some* people in *some* circumstances continue to feel a strong sense of attachment to a wider group, linked in personal history to socialization. This might explain why, in an inventive study, Gil-White suggested that evidence indicates that many people do indeed see their ethnic identities as 'primordial' (Gil-White 1999).

Summary: primordial ethnic groups

The term 'primordial' was in its original formulation a perfectly intelligible distinction between civic and non-civic ties, the civic being those ties associated with citizenship and citizen-like obligations in a modern state. By contrast primordial ties were those deriving from birth into a particular family, community, religious or language group. Birth into and experience of living in these primary groups brings with it a complex of attitudes and cultural dispositions. In this sense the primordial–civic distinction was similar to a familiar range of sociological distinctions such as 'universalistic and particularistic' (see Parsons 1968) or between *Gemeinschaft* and *Gesellschaft* (Tönnies 1963). These distinctions are highly schematic; but few would deny that something is being discerned as a real distinction between relationships which have a certain 'given' or ascribed quality and relationships which are ordered by contractual considerations, by 'interest', or by the regulatory principles of states and formal organizations.

In the field of ethnicity the difficulty began when some writers began speaking as if 'primordiality' was viewed as a characteristic of ethnic ties. This was then translated into a 'primordial' conceptualization of ethnic groups (or ethnicity) as against other conceptualizations, mostly characterized as 'instrumental' and 'circumstantial'. This is a wholly mistaken debate and its protagonists, above all Eller and Coughlan, appear to have seriously 'missed the point' or addressed something quite different from those they claim to criticize. In the end Eller and Coughlan appear to want to deny, not the existence of primordiality as a quality of ethnic groups, but the existence of primordiality at all (Eller and Coughlan 1993). That is, to 'think out of existence' primordiality is somehow to turn one's back on affect, the powerful influence of familiarity and customariness in social life, and the diffuse sense of attachment that flows from circumstances of birth and socialization, use of language and ingrained habits of thought and social practice.

To speak of this kind of 'customariness', 'familiarity', 'conventions of language and thought' and the like is not to invoke an unexplored and unexplorable realm of irrationality in human behaviour, and certainly not to imply that 'irrationality and affect' are dominant forces in social life (cf. Bourdieu 1990). It is simply to acknowledge that this kind of familiarity exists, that habits of thought do become ingrained and are often associated with early life, place, the family, and wider grouping or regions. Those who originally made the distinction between civic and primordial ties were making precisely this point – and not describing ethnic groups as 'primordial'. It is perfectly possible to have a conception of ethnic groups which allows us to see them – or more abstractly, to see ethnic ties or ethnicity – as being constituted by elements which are civic, instrumental, circumstantial and primordial. In plain terms the question of the primordiality of ethnic ties is one for exploration, not definition. A model of ethnicity which pre-ordains ethnically oriented action (or ethnic group membership, ethnic politics) as instrumental (circumstantial, situational) or as affective will be evading the difficulties.

5
Key Points in the Ethnicity Literature

After introducing the terms 'race', 'nation' and 'ethnic group' we looked at some key sociologists who used the term 'ethnic groups'. We also took quite a close look at the debate about 'primordialism' which provided an entrée into raising questions about the nature of ethnic attachments. It was in the 1960s with their publication *Beyond the Melting Pot*, and subsequently in 1975 with *Ethnicity: Theory and Experience* that Nathan Glazer and Daniel Moynihan began to popularize the term 'ethnicity'. As we have suggested, a discourse of ethnicity began to challenge, partly combine with and partly replace a discourse of race. We referred to Hirschman et al. (2000) speculating that the term '*ethnicity* eventually may supplant *race*' whilst conceding that in the USA race terminology remains dominant in official categorizations and popular discourse. If we look more closely at the original Glazer and Moynihan contributions we can see how some of the main aspects of the 'discourse of ethnicity' took shape. In this chapter we shall look back at these early works as well as looking at how these works are now regarded at the beginning of the twenty-first century; in the latter task we are able to draw on a retrospective symposium.

We shall take a critical look at two other important sources. In a famous collection of essays (1969), published in the same decade as Glazer and Moynihan's work, Fredrik Barth made a lasting contribution to the way we think about ethnicity. And in *Racial Formation in the United States*, Omi and Winant (1986) were sceptical about the ethnicity framework, and made their case for regarding 'racial formation' as *a*, if not *the*, central form of the structuring of US society.

Glazer and Moynihan: ethnicity, a new term, a new phenomenon?

As we have noted, the *Oxford English Dictionary* cites the earliest use of a noun 'ethnicity' – as against 'ethnic groups' and other adjectival uses – as 1953, but there is little doubt that the writings of Glazer and Moynihan in the 1960s and 1970s in America had the effect of making the term popular, or at least well used, among academics and in the press and general discourse. Their first book was published in 1963 (and reprinted with a new introduction in 1970) under the title *Beyond the Melting Pot: The Negroes, Puerto Ricans, Jews, Italians, and Irish of New York City*. The second (1975), *Ethnicity: Theory and Experience*, was an edited collection, to which they contributed the introductory essay, widely cited since that time as setting out some now-familiar positions about ethnicity. After introducing and discussing the principal themes we shall also examine a notable revisiting of their work. In spring 2000, '35 years on', in the journal *International Migration Review*, a group of scholars evaluated anew the early Glazer and Moynihan work (Alba 2000; E. Anderson 2000; Foner 2000; Glazer 2000; Kasinitz 2000).

The first of the two books uses the term 'ethnicity' but only as a description of the area of interest. The 1975 volume contains an essay on the theme of ethnicity as a 'new thing'. The principal theme of the 1963 book was that ethnic identities had survived in a way that previous generations of sociologists, such as Park and Warner for example, had not expected. Warner had thought that ethnic groups would fade because of the power of assimilation to mainstream American culture. Racial groups would endure because of the fixed valuation of racial difference on the part of the white majority. However, Glazer and Moynihan did not mean that ethnic cultures, of language, dress, religion, food and marriage pref-

erences, had somehow survived the onslaught of Americanization against all the odds. Their main argument in the first
volume is that ethnic groups have survived *despite cultural
change within them*, change largely in the direction of
Americanization.

Ethnic groups then, even after distinctive language, customs and
culture are lost, as they largely were in the second generation, and
even more fully in the third generation, are continually recreated by
new experiences in America. The mere existence of a name itself is
perhaps sufficient to form group character in new situations, for the
name associates an individual with a certain past, country, race. But
... a man is connected to his group by ties of family and friend-
ship. But he is also connected by ties of interest. The ethnic groups
in New York are also interest groups. This is perhaps the single most
important fact about ethnic groups in New York city. (Glazer and
Moynihan 1963, p. 17)

There was a certain ethnic pattern of residential concentrations, which combined with a pattern of occupational and
social class concentrations. Thus we see, for example, 'Black
New Yorkers in Harlem in low paid service employment';
'Italians', they write, 'means homeowners in Staten Island,
the North Bronx, Brooklyn and Queens'. These combinations
and concentrations produce a real social basis for ethnic
identifications. This also meant that politicians could
appeal explicitly or tacitly to these constituencies so that by
showing sympathy for 'people like you', i.e. living in this area,
having this sort of income, having this kind of accent, a
politician might target the Irish or Italian vote. The end of
the above quotation cites this ethnic–class combination
as 'the most important' fact that they have observed, suggesting that it goes a long way towards explaining this apparently unexpected turn of events, the survival of ethnic
identities.

But, as Banks has also observed (Banks 1996), in retrospect one of the most remarkable features about *Beyond the
Melting Pot* was its republication in 1970 with an introduction to the second edition. Curiously, Glazer and Moynihan
appear in places to have forgotten their earlier demotion of
'culture'. The book had asserted, they write, that 'ethnicity

remains important; it would continue to be important for politics and culture' (p. vii); just a little later they refer to 'ethnic groups . . . defined by common culture as well as common descent' (p. xiv). This is rather different from their previous emphasis on the persistence of ethnicity despite 'Americanization' and on the grounding of ethnic identities in class and community realities. In fact the 'class' argument is sustained in the second edition's introduction, if not as emphatically. But these are not the main shifts to be found in the revisionist comments of that introduction.

One of the main shifts comes in their revision of their understanding of a group which they, and others, still referred to as 'Negroes'. 'That Negroes were, or were becoming, one group in a society made up of self-conscious groups was the basic assumption of the book' (introduction to the second – 1970 – edition of *Beyond the Melting Pot*). They were one among many ethnic groups, seen not as the descendants of a former slave population with 350 years of history in America, but as immigrants to New York, albeit from the South. Indeed they tend to treat the South as another country, rein-forcing the notion that Negroes were immigrants like Polish immigrants from Europe. So in New York, with its openness to immigrants, 'the larger experience of the Negro would be overcome, as the Negroes joined the rest of society, in con-flict and accommodation, as an ethnic group' (p. xiii).

By 1970 they appear to accept that this presentation of 'Negroes' as an ethnic group based on immigration to the great American city would not hold. 'As an ethnic group they would be one of many. As a "racial group", as "blacks" as the new nomenclature has it, they would form a unique group in American society' (p. xiii), and since the ethnic categories did not work, 'we seem to be moving to a new set of cat-egories, black and white, and that is ominous'.

There can be little doubt that this startling re-assessment of this part of their 1963 thesis was a consequence of events intervening between 1963 and 1970. This was the age of the rise of Black Power (Carmichael 1976), the emergence of the Black Panther Party and the occurrence of serious disorders in many American cities, not least in the wake of the assas-sination of the African American leader Martin Luther King. Black militancy provoked in Glazer and Moynihan a considerable measure of disapproval, and, it seems, bitterness and anger. A couple of examples will illustrate their reaction to black militancy and support for it among white radicals. In commenting on the non-negotiable nature of militant demands they write: '[this] ignored that other groups did have interests, did have power, and would and could react against militant and arrogant demands which owed to the black culture of the streets a good deal of their peculiar bite and arrogance'; and 'verbal abuse has become the only form [of conducting business] as far as black militants are concerned, with the encouragement of the white intelligentsia'.

Later in the new introduction they reconstruct a discussion between 'black radicals' and an employer who is telling them that others have waited many years for chances of promotion and better jobs. They have the black speaker saying: 'Do you expect Negroes to wait that long for a good job?' There is, Glazer and Moynihan write, an answer to this question: 'Everyone else has.' Glazer and Moynihan start counting from when black Americans migrated to New York (from the late nineteenth, early twentieth century onwards), not from when they migrated from Africa to the British New World colonies, up to 400 years before – quite a long wait.

In summary, they conclude that an ethnic model was only partially successful. 'We, black and white, continue to grapple with *our primal dilemma*, the place of blacks in American society' (p. xxii, my emphasis). The quotations above suggest that they reach this conclusion with no little irritation and displeasure.

The new introduction (1970) rehearses the possible causes of this persistence of ethnicity. In part it may be attributable to the decline of other identities, among them religious and occupational identifications. Despite the fact they had argued for a link between ethnic identities and class and residential communities, they lean here towards seeing ethnic identities as *replacing* class identities, a theme to be replayed many times subsequently. But they also entertain, and then reject, another and rather ominous possibility. This is the possibility that the 'white' ethnic identities, Polish, Irish, Italian, Jewish and the like, are a tacit or coded statement of white interests and views of the world in relation to 'threats' from the black population.

In a word is the resurgence of ethnicity simply a matter of the resurgence of racism, as is now often asserted? Is the reaction of whites, of ethnic groups and the working and middle class, to the increasingly militant demands of Negroes a matter of defence of ethnic and occupational turfs and privileges or is it a matter of racial antipathy . . . and racism? (p. xxxviii)

Glazer and Moynihan conclude that this is not an adequate explanation. The ethnicity of the white ethnics cannot be dismissed as racism. What the Irish think and feel as Irish Americans (rather than as white Americans) is not a subterfuge, it is real: 'ethnicity is a real and felt basis of political and social action' (p. xxxviii). This is a shift of emphasis in other key respects. Ethnicity here is not merely 'instrumental', that is, a search for political and material gains under an ethnic banner. It is 'real' and is a basis for 'social' action, not just political action. This is to see ethnicity as being significant in much broader terms than the original argument.

'Something new has appeared'

By 1975 Glazer and Moynihan, this compelling pairing of a classic American liberal academic with an academic-cum-policy-maker who had served in Nixon's administration, were publishing again. *Ethnicity: Theory and Experience* was a collection of essays reporting on world-wide contexts of ethnic conflict, politics and society, with a long introductory essay by the editors. Ethnicity seems to be a new thing, they write, and not just a new term. This is not an intellectual fashion; rather, 'Something new has appeared' (p. 2) and this is 'the emergence of a new social category as significant for the understanding of the present-day world as that of social class itself'. This new phenomenon is 'the pronounced and sudden increase in tendencies by people in many countries and in many circumstances to insist on the significance of their group distinctiveness and identity and on new rights that derive from this group character'.

   Furthermore, this importance of ethnic groups has extended beyond minorities to '*all the groups of a society* characterised by a distinct sense of difference owing to culture and descent' (p. 4; my emphasis). The consequence is that 'ethnicity' becomes a leading tool for analysis of societies in their totality *because it embraces everyone*:

> A new word reflects a new reality. The new word is ethnicity and the new usage is the steady expansion of the term 'ethnic group' from minority and marginal subgroups at the edges of society – groups expected to assimilate, to disappear, to continue as survivals, exotic or troublesome – to major elements of a society. (p. 5)

Thus in the United States, they suggest, even old Americans, 'descendants of Anglo-Saxons', are considered an ethnic group.

These groups are still seen, as they were in the former volume, as interest groups, who lobby and make material claims on behalf of their members. They argue that ethnicity is a more powerful identification than class and this is because classes are all 'normatively' the same – they all want, in the words of the American trade unionist Samuel Gompers, the same thing: more. But they say 'ethnic differences *are* differences, or at least are seen as such' (p. 15). But if ethnic groups are interest groups it is not just because they form communities (in, for example, New York City) with broadly shared areas of residence, pattern of life, and class position. It is also because ethnicity has become a governmental principle for allocating resources: 'The strategic efficacy of ethnicity as a basis for asserting claims against government has its counterpoint in the seeming ease whereby government employs ethnic categories as a basis for distributing its rewards' (p. 10). This they view as a reversal of the 'colour-blindness' of the civil rights legislation which outlawed the use of 'ascriptive categories' as a basis of distribution. But 'within hours of the enactment of the statute in 1964' government began to require the recording of sex and race categories in all major institutions as a form of ethnic monitoring. This was both to gauge the progress of anti-discriminatory measures and to match services to groups, providing personnel of the same cultural, ethnic and racial backgrounds as their clients: 'Azerbaijani junky, Azerbaijani counsellor', they suggest.

Glazer and Moynihan in retrospect

The two books here considered are worthy of extended consideration not so much because of their own merit – the authors admit that they are 'not sure' on many things – but because they have been so widely influential and because they raised questions which remain central to the problematic of ethnicity. We can review just what those questions and suggested answers were, in the Glazer and Moynihan view of the world.

Ethnicity: new word, new reality

The persistence of ethnicity is a newly recognized phenomenon. This is not the failure of older cultures to change but their continuation in new forms in new contexts – such as third-generation Italians in New York. And it is not just New York (as in Glazer and Moynihan's 1963 book), or just in the USA, it is everywhere (1975). It has defied the 'liberal expectancy' of assimilation to new civic cultures and obstructed the demise of 'ascriptive' ties and identities. But Glazer and Moynihan show some hesitation about this, not quite convinced that we are entering a new world of ethnicity. They do refer to symbolic ethnicity – ethnic identities with the cultural difference stripped out. This is a term developed by Herbert Gans to describe a situation in which ethnic identities persisted despite the diminution of cultural difference. Glazer and Moynihan suggest that '*to this extent the liberal expectancy was right*' (my emphasis).

Instrumental ethnicity

Glazer and Moynihan's essays have been seen as a reference point for the instrumental view of ethnicity (cf. Banks 1966) whereby ethnically informed action is opportunist, in pursuit of particular goals which can be achieved through maximizing ethnic identities. This is in contrast to a view of ethnic groups as profound and organic bases of social and cultural difference. Certainly the interest-group argument is repeated throughout and there is, in places, a view of ethnic groups as quasi-classes. But again this is not consistent. Even though they suggest that American ethnic groups have become Americanized they also speak of ethnic groups as 'distinctive' and of a sense of difference 'owing to culture and descent'.

State-sponsored ethnicity

The significant addition to Glazer and Moynihan's second volume is the idea that ethnic interests can be pursued in relation to the state. Once the state takes a hand in using ethnic categories to allocate resources it both creates or confirms ethnic categories and makes ethnicity a politically instrumental principle. The 'Azerbaijani' remark suggests they were not impressed. The actions of the state in defining ethnic groups and in regulating rights, privileges and prohibitions along ethnic lines, is at least as important as relations between individuals and collectivities along ethnic lines.

Race and ethnicity

The continuing significance of 'race' in general but of American 'black–white' relations in particular causes Glazer and Moynihan to reconsider their view that the concept of ethnicity could subsume or supersede 'race'. This agonizing over the dogged and bitter persistence of the so-called 'colour line' in the USA was most evident in the 1970 introduction; they seem decidedly shaken by events between 1963 and 1970 in America's cities. By 1975 their anxieties have receded and they say little about it. The volume's chapter on African Americans speaks of 'neo-ethnicity' and 'political ethnicity' (the word 'Negroes' still appears in this book but it is giving way to 'Blacks'. 'Afro-Americans' makes an appearance, but not yet 'African Americans').

Minorities and majorities

One of the great departures from earlier work, of their own and of others, in Glazer and Moynihan's 1975 volume is the reference to majority ethnicity. In America and elsewhere 'ethnic groups' were viewed as minorities or as smaller and particular groups within a larger whole. The majority population were not considered to have ethnic attributes, just the attributes of 'us' as 'most people'; 'we' were what 'other people' were different from, not part of a total system of difference. This is in marked contrast to Lloyd Warner whom we discussed earlier. Putting it crudely, the question being raised was 'ethnicity – have we all got it?' and by 1975 Glazer and Moynihan are saying 'yes'.

These five issues, *the newness of ethnicity, instrumental ethnicity, ethnicity and the state, race and ethnicity*, and *majority ethnicity*, all remain central areas of contention in this field. In some cases our ways of thinking have moved on and clarified things; in other instances the facts have moved on. By and large, for example, the definition of ethnic groups as 'simply' cultural groups has been progressively abandoned, much influenced by Barth's important essay in 1969 (this is briefly mentioned by Glazer and Moynihan in 1975). Cultures, it is agreed, do not neatly coincide with ethnicities and ethnic groups cannot be identified primarily by cultural difference. Similarly the notion of majority ethnicity has been widely canvassed, although the popular association of 'ethnic' with minority, and with exotic otherness, persists.

But with respect to the issue which affects Glazer and Moynihan more than they seem ready to admit – race and racism in America – things moved on a great deal in the last quarter of the twentieth century. The headline name identifier, 'Americans of African descent', has moved on from Negroes, to Blacks, to Afro-Americans, to African Americans, a term which brings a kind of equivalence with other hyphenated terms whose first half is a country of origin (in this case a continent of origin). Other large groupings have assumed greater importance – and greater numbers – including Hispanics and Asian Americans, thus complicating the primary black–white division. On the other hand, the argument that 'blacks' disrupted the pattern of ethnicity (as Glazer and Moynihan were tending to argue) by bringing 'race' back in, has diminished in importance.

The discourse of race persists in America, side by side with a discourse of ethnicity as we showed in chapter 1. The two authors may need now to rethink their argument that white ethnicity was not capable of being understood as a response to black demands. This interpretation of white ethnicity has gained ground (see Waters 1990). As Waters argues (p. 164), 'This analysis suggests both that symbolic ethnicity persists because it meets a need Americans have for community without individual cost and that a potential societal cost of this symbolic ethnicity is in its subtle reinforcement of racism.' One undertone, at least, of white 'ethnics' reviving interests in their origins is that it was in response to black ethnicity. 'If you can do it, so can we' was the message. Glazer and Moynihan's own essay in 1975 edges towards such a view when they refer to state dispensation of resources. The civil rights legislation brought in its train necessary procedures designed to measure ethnic access to resources. Once this was the case ethnic identities took on a new importance. As they themselves argue, the civil rights legislation abolished the civic significance of race and almost at the same moment invented procedures for monitoring and implementing the wish for greater factual equality. This prompted large proportions of the population to take an unexpected interest in their group identities.

A critique of ethnicity

Through the writings of Glazer and Moynihan the sociological interest in ethnicity in the USA was much advanced. There is one important contribution in particular which has raised serious doubts about how a 'paradigm of ethnicity' has been deployed in the USA. This is Michael Omi and Howard Winant's *Racial Formation in the United States, from the 1960s to the 1980s*, first published in 1986. Despite being a critique of ethnicity as a model in sociology, much of what is argued is entirely consonant with what we have argued in this book. Most notably Omi and Winant were among the first to argue quite explicitly for the proposition that the categories of race and the accompanying ideological constructions (that is, politically accented ideas about racial groups) were to be understood as socially and politically constructed. They are therefore quite sure that the category 'race', with its implication of fixed inherited and biologically structured difference, cannot be defended. In this sense they accept a paradigm of 'race' which precisely shares the argument about social construction that we have pursued here.

The meaning of race is defined and contested throughout society, in both collective action and personal practice. In the process, racial categories themselves are formed, transformed, destroyed and reformed. We use the term racial formation to refer to the process by which social, economic and political forces determine the content and importance of racial categories, and by which they are in turn shaped by racial meanings. (Omi and Winant 1986, p. 61)

This statement presents racial categories as being socially 'constructed' or 'formed' and it argues that the *determining* forces are 'social, economic and political forces'. The point of departure appears to centre upon the idea of 'irreducibility'. In social science the term 'reductionism' (reducible, irreducible) usually refers to an idea of hierarchy of explanation. If, for example, A explains B, then A is seen as being 'above' B in a hierarchy of explanation. In this way the emphasis on A is seen to be 'undermining' the status of B and treating it as somehow less important – because its place in social structure, or indeed in history, is dependent on A. In this respect Omi and Winant's book is a plea for a much more central place for 'race' in American social thought. This too corresponds to much of what we have argued in this book; it seems indisputable that a discourse of race has been and remains more firmly embedded in US society than almost anywhere else.

The general question of causation is, however, more difficult. A better model of explanation is to propose that A and B are in some way bound up with each other rather than to suggest that A causes B or the reverse. At first (see the above quotation about social forces) this seems close to what Omi and Winant are proposing. But this very quotation (from which I had purposely left off the next sentence) is followed by this argument:

Crucial to this formulation is the treatment of race as a central axis of social relations which cannot be subsumed under or reduced to some broader category of conception. (pp. 61–2)

This statement reads as a reversal of the reductionist direction, that no reality in American history can over-ride the realities of race – or racism. However difficult this would be to 'prove', the theme is undoubtedly a principal one in *Racial Formation*. Class theories – and it would seem well nigh impossible to detach American racism from the class history and class formation of US society – are viewed by Omi and Winant as understating race and even as foreign to the USA: 'Often influenced by movements and traditions *whose reference points were located outside the US*, many radical perspectives simply fail to address specific US conditions' (p. 3, my emphasis).

Their main concern, though, remains the one of 'irreducibility'. In their words they are concerned 'to locate race at the center of American political history . . . to emphasize . . . the irreducible political aspects of racial dynamics' (p. 4). It is notable that they speak of the centrality of 'race', rather than the centrality of racism. The implication is that to abandon a discourse in which 'race' is a central term is to abandon something crucial. It is their critique of 'ethnicity' which exposes just what this something is.

The part of their book which addresses the ethnicity paradigm makes it clear that their objections are not to the sociology of ethnicity in general *but to the specific assumptions which they believe are constitutive elements of ethnicity theory in the USA*. In short, those who are concerned with 'ethnicity' in the USA have made insupportable assumptions about the direction to be taken by ethnic groups (races) in the USA. The two most important, and false, assumptions they detect are these: that assimilation into an American mainstream is the long-term likely outcome for all ethnic groups in the USA, including African Americans, and that in making this assumption they are assuming that African Americans can be regarded in accordance with the same paradigm as immigrants from Europe and their descendants. 'Ethnicity theory assigned to blacks and other racial minority groups the roles which earlier generations of European immigrants had played ... But ... structural barriers continued to render the immigrant analogy inappropriate' (p. 20). This approach, they argue, is 'a neglect of race *per se*', and again this is stated as a neglect of 'race' not of racism. But from all this we can distil two principal arguments. The first is that it is incorrect to treat the position of black Americans as analogous to that of immigrants from Europe, and the second is that to do so is to assume a relatively uniform pattern of assimilation and social mobility and thus to neglect the special importance of racism. It is because what Omi and Winant call 'ethnicity theory' in the USA incorporates these errors that they reject it. What an immigration model neglects is the sheer power and intensity of white USA's resistance to the incorporation and social mobility of black people (cf. Fenton 1999). In the symposium held more than thirty years after the publication of *Beyond the Melting Pot* (by some referred to as BMP) some of these errors were recognized.

BMP thirty-five years on

One of the sources of error in Glazer and Moynihan's volume derived from their assumption that mass migration was at an end. As Nancy Foner eloquently shows, the idea that 'the cast of major characters for the next decades is complete' was a mistake. Instead mass migration has revived, with New York City alone receiving large numbers:

The newcomers are in the main from Asia, Latin America, and the Caribbean – and they continue to stream in at a rate of over 100,000 a year. In 1970, 18 percent of New York's residents were foreign born, a century low. By 1998, immigrants constituted over a third of the city's population, fast-approaching turn-of-the-century levels. (Foner 2000, p. 255)

It is generally agreed that these new immigrants may have complicated but not finally undermined the over-arching US black–white binary system. This is especially so, writes Foner, 'for West Indians who are often lumped with and suffer the same disabilities as African Americans – and for darker skinned Hispanics'. For white groups in the USA there has been a continuing steady process of assimilation into an American mainstream. Most of the authors in the review of *Beyond the Melting Pot* (*International Migration Review*, Spring 2000) seem to agree that the pot did do its melting, even if 'beyond the pot' some identities retained some salience. It was, however, a white pot: 'there is abundant evidence that assimilation is a process of major import, perhaps the master trend in fact, among whites in the US' (Alba and Nee 1997).

Much of the consciousness of ethnic origin among new non-white immigrants has been because of their awareness of racism towards American blacks: 'One reason many of today's immigrants stress their ethnic identity is that they want to distinguish themselves from native blacks and Puerto Ricans, the city's [New York] two most stigmatized minorities' (Foner 2000, p. 259).

Two other mistakes were made in the BMP volume, and acknowledged in the review, even by one of its authors. The first was to underestimate the power of racist principles in the USA, or to believe that the civil rights advances of the 1960s would continue rather than lose ground. There has been backward movement for black Americans in both the political and economic realms:

Politicians are gaining clout by proving themselves hostile to the advancement of blacks. Today we are experiencing the transformation of American cities from centers of manufacturing to centers of service and high technology. The loss of well-paying manufacturing jobs . . . has devastated the black working class. (E. Anderson 2000, p. 267)

Glazer's own observations included commenting that their BMP observations on black protests had been 'overwrought' and wrong in tone. But above all he suggests 'there was one further assumption that in retrospect appears wrong', namely in treating 'the newly expanded African American and Puerto Rican populations as immigrant populations'.

Cultures and boundaries

Briefly mentioned in Glazer and Moynihan's 1975 edited volume was the work of Fredrik Barth, the Norwegian anthropologist, whose writings have been singularly influential in the study of ethnicity. Barth's essay, published in 1969, was written as the introductory piece in a volume of collected essays deriving from a conference at Bergen in 1967 (Barth 1969). Two of the contributors write about peasant or nomadic communities in Norway; the others are concerned with ethnic identities in Sudan, Ethiopia, Mexico, Pakistan, Afghanistan and Laos. The central proposition coming out of Barth's work is that ethnic identities are sustained by the maintenance of what he calls 'boundaries', the lines which mark off one group from another. These lines are not drawn by simple cultural difference – e.g. the 'A's are the people who speak 'A'-language. The boundaries are drawn by social behaviour which is relevant to the recognition of membership, and to the drawing of distinctions; the cultural 'items' which are used to make this distinction vary, and may be only a small part of the cultural repertoire of a particular group. This could be stated as the proposition that: the 'A's are the people who are not 'B's; and speaking 'A'-language is a way of knowing and showing this. Indeed on Barth's argument the decisively important culture difference might be quite small (compared to, say, a major language difference).

Despite the fact that these insights were drawn from – for the most part – work grounded in 'Third World' societies, the relevance of Barth's central proposition has been taken to have general application. The kinds of segmentary societies – societies and collectivities with a distinctive way of life which are largely self-reproducing but lack a formal central authority – that Barth is discussing are often found in post-colonial societies straddling the geography of neighbouring states (such as Pathans in Pakistan and Afghanistan). As these post-colonial states attempt to secure their power and command over diverse populations, these segments are at risk. If they do not constitute part of a majority population or of a politically dominant elite, minorities distinguishable by a feature of language or religion find themselves under suspicion. Furthermore, where new states are weak, both economically and in the command of their territory, rivalries between contiguous groups or groups side by side in the same region may prove beyond the capacity of the state to control and restrain. Such groups, many of them in parts of Africa and Asia, are of the kind traditionally studied by anthropologists, such as Evans-Pritchard (1962) in the colonial era, by Edmund Leach (1982) rather later, and by Barth and his colleagues at the point of decolonization and beyond. For Barth, the Pathans of Pakistan and Afghanistan are an 'ethnic group'; for Glazer and Moynihan, the descendants of Italian immigrants in New York City are. The extent to which these are quite different ways of life in utterly different settings has not stopped people from discussing 'ethnicity' in both as if it were the same sort of phenomenon, wherever it might be found.

Barth begins by outlining how anthropologists typically define ethnic groups, citing four lines of definition:

1 A group which is largely self-perpetuating;
2 A group which shares fundamental cultural values;
3 A group which makes up a field of communication and interaction;
4 A group which has a membership which identifies itself and is identified by others as constituting a category distinguishable from other categories of the same order.

Barth does not dismiss any of the conventional meanings of the above but he is at pains to make it clear that it is not possible to define an ethnic group as the 'possessor' of a particular culture which functions to make it distinctive. The more he pursues his case the more he inclines to identifying 'social organization' as the definitive feature, and feature '4' above as the decisive one:

We can assume no one-to-one relationship between ethnic units and cultural similarities and differences. The features that are taken into account are not the sum of 'objective' differences but only those which the actors themselves regard as significant – some cultural features are used by actors as signals and emblems of difference, others are ignored. (p. 14)

It is not that culture is unimportant nor that there cannot be found real patterns of cultural difference. Barth speaks of overt signals or signs, including dress, language, house-form and lifestyle as well as moral values and standards. But the critical thing in defining the ethnic group is the 'maintenance of the boundary' between one group and another. The culture of a group may change or, in Barth's own words, 'be transformed' (p. 14), and the cultural item which marks 'A's from 'B's may be changed. Nonetheless the 'A's and 'B's persist. This leads Barth to his most succinct definition of this approach, the one subsequently most repeated: 'The critical focus of investigation from this point of view becomes the ethnic boundary that defines the group, not the cultural stuff which it encloses' (p. 15).

Having established a way of thinking about ethnic groups, Barth proceeds to examine how members of ethnic groups may behave both individually and collectively. Within an ethnic group, behaviours are construed differently from behaviour which crosses ethnic boundaries. With other members with whom identity is shared there is, as Barth puts it, an 'acceptance that both are playing the same game'. When this is so it makes it possible for their relationship 'to cover all different sectors and domains of activity'. Their relationship is not, in another sociological way of describing relationships, single-stranded. A relationship, for example a trading relationship in which 'A's exchange things with 'B's, is single-stranded if outside the trading exchange the 'A's have little or nothing to do with the 'B's. Thus, as Barth puts it, 'a dichotomization of others as strangers implies a recognition of limitations on shared understandings and a restriction of interaction to sectors of common understanding and mutual interest' (p. 15).

Barth's emphasis on identification of members and strangers, on the system of classification, on 'boundaries', and on the common understandings which govern relationships has been taken up by subsequent anthropologists (cf. Banks 1996 and particularly Eriksen 1993). These common understandings govern relationships between members, between members and strangers, and the scope of the relationships between members and strangers (for example, do they just trade with each other, or do they engage with each other in many ways?). But the most striking consequence of Barth's (quite short) essay has been to detach 'culture' from ethnic group.

Culture

We began this book by showing how all three principal concepts that are of interest to students of ethnicity – race, ethnic group and nation – have strong connotations of two attributes: descent and culture. We suggested that all three, race, nation, ethnic group, may be regarded, in broad terms, as 'descent and culture communities'. They are all forms of social identity, forms of inclusion and exclusion, forms of social classification, and modes of social interaction in which culture and descent are always implicated. We then suggested that if 'culture and descent' is the core of these concepts, in the particular elaborations of the concepts there are some key striking ways in which they depart from each other. Race, for example, has a long historical connection with heritable physical traits, with phenotypical difference, and also with an abstract theory of the divisions of humankind, albeit one that is much discredited. Nation has particularly strong connotations with claims to self-rule and is closely linked to the 'state' in the pairing as nation-state. It is also possible to detach the idea of nation entirely from the concept of shared ethnicity. If all-comers (at least those legitimately in-migrating) are welcomed as citizens and the multi-ethnic origins of a society are accepted, then the idea – or ideal – of the nation equates to a civic ideal of 'the citizens of the country'. This idea of nation is legally and constitutionally defined, not ethnically defined. Ethnic group by contrast has a history which has gathered up connotations of both foreignness and minority status, a 'group' less than the society as a whole. This connotation too has been weakened by the extension of the idea of ethnicity to majority ethnicity in Glazer and Moynihan and beyond.

But at this point we are making a mental note of the partial detachment of 'ethnic group' from culture. This detachment from culture is a departure from a 'traditional' sociological and anthropological idea of ethnic groups as marked by, and defined by, cultural difference. The detachment from culture has taken at least three forms. One is the Barthian argument: cultures associated with specific groups (e.g. Pathans in Pakistan and Afghanistan) may change and the elements of culture which are seen to mark them off from others are usually only a few items from the whole. A second is the Glazer and Moynihan argument: that ethnic groups (in the USA) *have* become more and more like each other in culture and behaviour; the language, religion and kinship customs which once marked them off have disappeared or lost their force, but the ethnic identities have persisted. This is similar to what Gans described as symbolic ethnicity (1979) and later symbolic religion (1994). The third is that where cultural difference is used as the mark of difference its claim to be ancestral culture is (or may be seen to be) shallow or unwarranted – what has been termed the 'invention of tradition' (Hobsbawm and Ranger 1983). None of this should deflect us from seeing that ethnicity and culture are closely implicated with each other. But this also reminds us that the way in which culture relates to, or defines, ethnicity is nothing like as straightforward as has sometimes been believed.

Summary: culture, race and ethnicity – symbolic ethnicity, power and choice

The discussion of Glazer and Moynihan's work, of Omi and Winant's intervention, of the retrospective evaluation of *Beyond the Melting Pot*, and of the implications of Barth's noted essay, all formed the themes of this chapter. Taken together they point towards some tentative conclusions.

The equation of 'ethnic group' with 'culture difference' has to be qualified (see above). It may seem like common sense to say that ethnic groups are the 'envelopes' containing culture difference but the Barthian emphasis on 'group boundaries' rather than 'cultural content' reverses this argument. The idea of culture difference tends towards a classificatory idea of ethnic groups (the 'A's are the people who do this, believe that, speak 'A'-language). The group boundary concept points towards a relational concept of ethnic groups (how do the 'A's know who the 'A's are and who the 'B's are, and how do they 'draw a line' between each other?). This Barthian emphasis does not discount the importance of cultural difference itself: where groups follow particular customs, adopt a familiar dress, and speak their own language, these things need to be studied and understood. They also become a means by which people are recognized. But the fact that a cultural item, such as language or dress, may function as a boundary marker does not mean that people do not also take the cultural item seriously. People do attach importance to customary dress and a familiar language; in multi-ethnic and multilingual societies, the defence of language rights comes to be seen as very important to group members. This 'intermediate' position on the importance of 'cultural content' as against 'boundary relations' is very well expressed by Stephen Cornell (Cornell 1996).

Two propositions flow from Omi and Winant's critique of the 'ethnicity discourse' in the United States. The first is that not all ethnic groups are in the same social structural position. The tendency to couple the idea of ethnicity with an expectation of assimilation and social mobility could not be applied equally to all ethnic groups in the USA. The mistake in Glazer and Moynihan was to ignore the structural and historic difference in the circumstances of African American and European immigrant incorporation into the USA. African American experience has been subjected to the binary white–black ethnic boundary which is superimposed on the African American and European immigrant boundary. Although ethnic differences among black Americans are important, these differences are typically ignored by others (Waters 1999). Furthermore the American case is an indication (as are many other cases) that ethnicity is not just about 'difference' but about structural inequality and a hierarchy of difference. As the politics of culture in the USA illustrates, culture differences are not 'mere' differences. They are also hierarchically ordered and unequally valued (Hollinger 1995; Steinberg 2000).

This chapter also introduced us to the idea of 'symbolic ethnicity' (Gans 1979). In this Gans drew upon evidence that ethnic identities persisted even when the 'cultural difference' which is often viewed as the 'content' of this ethnicity has itself very much diminished. In a word, people who regard themselves as 'Polish Americans' may have lost much or most of their Polishness but hold on to a Polish identity. This model renders ethnic identity as essentially 'optional'. But in many instances ethnic identities are far from optional. There is very little optional about Serbian and Kosovo Albanian relations. These are not mere 'symbolic ethnic identities' from which ethnic actors can opt out. Similarly in the USA there is more choice for some ethnic groups than for others. As Waters argued in her fascinating study *Ethnic Options* (Waters 1990, p. 156): 'The ways in which ethnicity is flexible and symbolic and voluntary for white middle class Americans are the very ways in which it is not so for non-white and Hispanic Americans.' This is precisely where the 'discourse of ethnicity' in the USA ends and the 'discourse of race' begins. Ethnic groups are 'voluntary' and choose their own boundaries; racial minorities are subject to the compelling actions of others. But whilst it is true that some people have more power, and more luxury of choice than others, it is not satisfactory to regard some people as primarily defined by the racism of others. The visible 'black–white' distinction is an important and powerful ethnic boundary and in the USA it is superimposed upon many other ethnic distinctions.

6
Migration, Ethnicity and Mobilization

The story so far

In chapters 1 through 4 the emphasis has been on seeking out the core meanings of the terms 'ethnic group', 'race' and 'nation'. We began chapter 1 with an etymological tracing which suggested that there is common ground across all three terms, and that they express the idea of a people, my people, or our people with shared origins. At the same time we showed what was distinctive about each term, marking one from the others. The term 'race' stands alone in being associated with a biological idea of divisions of humankind, now discredited sociologically but remaining powerful ideologically. From there, in chapter 2, we showed how in different countries and contexts there are variations in the 'local' discourses of race and ethnicity. In looking back at some key turning points in the development of a literature about ethnicity we saw how 'ethnic' terminology came partly to displace 'racial' terminology (see chapter 3), although in the USA 'races' are still described as measurable divisions of the population. Many writers in the USA argue that the social embeddedness of ideas about race is so powerful that sociologists should continue to use a 'race' terminology.

We also addressed (chapter 4) a principal debate in this field, the argument about the very nature of ethnicity as a 'primordial' identity. This was followed (in chapter 5) by a discussion of Glazer and Moynihan's study of New York in the 1960s which became a key point for the sociology of ethnicity, and introduced ideas of instrumental and political ethnicity. Another crucial departure was Barth's development of the idea of ethnic boundaries, the conceptualization of the way in which groups defined themselves as (culturally) different from others. In this first half of the book we also discussed the end-of-millennium revisiting of Glazer and Moynihan's book.

What is ethnicity, and how and when does it become important sociologically?

In rather an over-simplification we may regard the early chapters as discussing 'what is ethnicity?' and the second half of the book as asking, and answering, the question 'in what ways and under what circumstances does ethnicity become sociologically important?' We have defined ethnic identity as a communal and individual identity expressed as an idea of 'our people, our origins' which *clearly varies* in the intensity with which it is felt and expressed. There are features of ethnicity, as an important dimension of social relations, which appear again and again. As we have argued, one of these is a social construction of ancestry; a second is marks of culture and culturally constructed visible differences. Social (i.e. in social relationships) and societal (i.e. at the level of a society or nation-state) disputes over the protection and advancement of culture are a common way in which ethnicity is mobilized. Perhaps the commonest of these culture-protection struggles are those over language and religion in schooling. In Malaysia, for example, the preservation of Tamil-based primary schools is one way in which Malaysian Indians strengthen their identity. In England some groups are anxious to foster Islamic education, inside and outside the mainstream educational system (Rex 1996).

There is one clue to why, *when it is mobilized*, ethnic identity may be an apparently powerful source of action. This is because it can be, for the individual and the community, a totalizing identity: if people are concerned about their jobs, their neighbourhood, their education and that of their children, their legal status, their personal security, *under the right circumstances ethnic identity may be incorporated in all of these.* In other circumstances, ethnic identity may scarcely enter into the individual identity as a premise of action; indeed there may hardly be an ethnic identity at all, except some broad and diffuse category which barely seems to the individual to have any action significance. In between these poles are circumstances where ethnic identity is recognized and understood but evoked in only some situations, being irrelevant in others. Thus we may think of *totalizing ethnicities, nil* or *tacit ethnicities,* and *provisional ethnicities.* Totalizing ethnicities can be found when ethnic organization and ethnic attributions of meaning pervade all or almost all spheres of life. Under these circumstances ethnic identity is totalizing or summative – it draws in to itself everything else. Nil or tacit ethnicities can be found wherever there is some cultural material capable of giving rise to an ethnic identity, but to all intents and purposes it has no social significance. Provisional ethnicities are those which are more than tacit but the mobilization is occasional and contingent. Whether the ethnic identity takes on the form of one or another of these, depends to a great extent on social circumstances external to the individual. For example, if neighbourhoods are typically ethnically concentrated, then daily life is very much coloured by this; excursions outside the neighbourhood are experienced as 'departures'. If an ethnic group, or a group marked by ethnic features, is also overwhelmingly concentrated in an economic niche (such as all slaves, all traders), then the ethnic identity has an added social force.

Action and conditions of action

It is by using these sociological assumptions that we can adopt something like a choice theory of ethnically informed action. This is not an assertion that ethnically informed action is a simple consequence of choice by the actor (e.g. 'I wish to show that I am Irish, and I act accordingly'). And it is not simply an assertion that choosing to act in an ethnically informed way is a rational choice, that is some kind of instrumentality ('I wish to show that I am Irish, and I act accordingly because it suits me, and gets me where I want to go'). The circumstances in which people choose how to act (and in particular choose whether to act in accordance with ethnic principles) can be, and frequently are, pretty compelling. Whatever the private wish of the individual, it is submerged by the compelling constraint of one's fellow ethnic members, or by one's ethnic others. In the next chapters of this book our strategy is to examine some of the circumstances under which people may – or may not – act in accordance with an ethnic identity. The emphasis will be on the analysis of the circumstances as the conditions of action.

Thomas Eriksen (1993) identified some different contexts of ethnicity, a typology adopted and modified in *Ethnicity: Racism, Class and Culture* (Fenton 1999). Some of this schema is reproduced here.

Types and Contexts of Ethnicity

Migrant worker populations and their descendants, typically though not always in urban centres of rich countries; in the nineteenth century many people from Europe migrated to the United States, discharging European peasants into the USA's growing industrial economy; in the twentieth and twenty-first centuries, migrations have derived from and dispersed to many different regions, and are certainly not confined to plantation and industrial workers.

Plural groups, which were typically the legacy of colonial societies where large numbers of servile workers had been imported, often in 'preference' to the proletarianization of an indigenous population who remained in subsistence, peasant-producer, or marginal agricultural or homesteader economies; imported workers in some contexts replaced slave labour, originated in India, and worked and lived under conditions not much freer than slavery.

Post-slavery populations, of which those in Brazil, the USA and the Caribbean are best known; these movements of people were forced, unfree and typically linked to plantation economies (sugar, spice, coffee, pineapple, cotton, tobacco production); most New World enslaved peoples originated among populations of the West coast and interior of Africa.

Indigenous peoples overwhelmed and dispossessed by colonial settlers, organizing to restore their land and cultures as among Maori in New Zealand.

Ethno-nations, where the boundaries of modern nationhood, the state and group autonomy remained contested, usually where a nationalist political movement (as in Quebec in Canada, the Basque country in Spain: see Guiberneau 1999) aims to secede or gain a high degree of autonomy; territory, regional autonomy or independence are the key dimensions of ethno-nationalisms or 'nations without states' (Fenton and May 2002; McCrone 1998).

In this volume we will not explore all the possible contexts for the creation and mobilization of ethnic identities (see Fenton 1999). The last two tend to form quite special areas of study (see Ghai 2000; Guiberneau 1999; McCrone 1998; Fleras and Elliot 1992; Fleras and Spoonley 2000). The first three are all cases and consequences of labour migration, which vary from entirely free to entirely forced. Furthermore in most societies, the state not only controls in-migration (and in some cases out-migration) quite closely, but has a role in determining the status of immigrants and minorities. The importance of ethnicity in any society is partly influenced by the activities of the state, and the protection which the state does or does not provide. Many migrant workers, certainly including enslaved peoples, have had their lives defined by the fact that the state barely guarantees security and protection, let alone provides cultural and legal recognition. In chapters 6 and 7 we will discuss these particular themes – migration, ethnic mobilization, minority–majority relations, social mobility and identity – as key themes in the sociology of ethnicity.

Trends in world migration

Before turning directly to ethnicity in a migration context, we should take a brief look at world migration, a huge topic in its own right. Castles and Miller, with their *Age of Migration* (1993), have provided an invaluable guide to this topic, as does Castles in *Ethnicity and Globalisation* (2000). *Globalisation in Question* (Hirst and Thompson 1999) puts migration in a global economic setting. In the seventeenth to the nineteenth century, some 15 to 20 million people were transported from Africa into slavery in the New World. These were peoples with many different languages whose local and regional cultures were often submerged in the New World, to be replaced by syncretic cultures, religions and musical traditions from Brazil to Haiti to Jamaica and the American (USA) South.

In the nineteenth century the USA became a big target of immigrants, mostly from Europe, and in the first half of the century mostly from Britain:

The greatest era for recorded voluntary mass migration was the century after 1815. Around 60 million people left Europe for the Americas, Oceania and South and East Africa. An estimated 10 million voluntarily migrated from Russia to Central Asia and Siberia. A million went from Southern Europe to North Africa. About 12 million Chinese and 6 million Japanese left their homelands and emigrated to East and South Asia. One and a half million left India for South East Asia and South and West Africa. (Hirst and Thompson 1999, p. 23)

All commentators agree that the most recent decades have seen a globalization of migration, more countries involved than ever before as senders and receivers, with more people moving more quickly than in the past:

Of the world's estimated 80 million recent international migrants, a quarter are thought to be legally admitted workers, another quarter illegally resident aliens, one quarter spouses and children and the remainder, refugees and asylum seekers. (Castles and Miller 1993, p. 168)

International migration is part of a transnational revolution that is re-shaping societies and politics around the globe . . . areas like the United States, Canada, Australia, New Zealand, or Argentina are classical countries of immigration. Their populations consist mainly of European immigrants and their descendants. The aboriginal populations of these countries have been partially destroyed and dis-possessed; today the survivors have a marginal and discriminated experience. (Castles and Miller 1993, p. 5)

The world's non-voluntary migrants, as reported by the United Nations High Commission for Refugees (UNHCR) (January 2002), are rather differently distributed. Almost 20 million people are listed as 'Persons of concern who fall under the mandate of the UNHCR'. The regions with the largest numbers are Asia (8.8m), Europe (4.8m) and Africa (4.1m); smaller numbers are found in Northern America (1m), Latin America and the Caribbean (0.8m) and Oceania (80,000) (UNHCR 2002).

These refugees form about one fifth of the world's esti-mated 100 million migrants, and this total migrant popula-tion is estimated to be about 1.7 per cent of the world's population (Castles and Miller 1993, p. 4). The 'transna-tional revolution' of migration is accelerating, becoming more global, involving more countries as receiver and sender societies. For example, oil-rich Middle Eastern countries are now large in-migrant societies; the countries of southern Europe, particularly Greece, Italy, Spain and Portugal, his-torically exporters of people, have become receivers; Japan has a growing immigrant population, and Malaysia has a large part of its agricultural labour force from neighbouring Indonesia. Transnational migration increases and so do transnational communities.

Migrants and plural societies

Those societies often discussed as post-colonial or plural soci-eties (Rex 1973, 1996; Fenton 1999) have inherited a legacy of cultural difference. Many of those who now form the basis of ethnic difference in post-colonial societies travelled to their new countries in the latter part of the nineteenth century and the early twentieth. Indians in Malaysia would be a good example, of plantation workers imported in the early twen-tieth century. The decisive change in the significance of ethnicity in comparable (i.e. comparable in the sense of receiving Indian workers) post-colonial societies such as Sri Lanka, Fiji, Guyana, Trinidad and Malaysia came with political independence in the 1960s. Then the economic and political basis of people's engagement in the social whole was transformed. People saw their individual lives as tied up with the direction taken by the state and as capable of influence by their political participation. The colonial order had at least partially insulated members of different groups from each other, as occupants of different niches in the economy. They were barely implicated in the political system, dominated as it was by the ruling power, which was in all the above cases, the British. With the advent of democratic politics and greater individual mobility within the economy, the process of individuation or detachment from group allegiances may begin. The question then becomes: how far does this process of individuation go? Can people be detached from collective obligations and collective identities which have been the acknowledged or tacit basis of security in the recent past? In most cases the first results of democratic politics are to harden ethnic identities. In democratic contest politics, tacit identities become politically explicit and in competition.

This is why so many observers thought that they detected an 'ethnic revival' in the 1960s and 1970s, the period of decolonization and the first decades of competitive politics in post-colonial regimes. Of course there was no ethnic revival in the sense that forgotten communities and identities somehow miraculously revived. Established, and grounded in everyday life, tacit identities became significant in a new way, in the explicit identities of a competitive political sphere, which had the capacity to affect people's ability to sustain their ways of living. This was the way ethnicities often worked in post-colonial societies which managed to maintain democratic politics (even if with difficulty), such as Malaysia, Sri Lanka and Fiji (see Horowitz 1989). All individuals in the new democratic (independent) state are now actors in the political system but the history of communal solidarity and separateness mean that this participation is via communal identities. The new state aims to create a new nation, incorporating and to some extent over-riding particular communities. This has been achieved to a degree in Malaysia (Milne and Mauzy 1999), clearly not so in Fiji (Lawson 1992, 1997). In other, but despotic and corrupt, post-colonial regimes ethnic politics may remain concealed but then erupt when the central power weakens or collapses, as in Indonesia in the 1990s.

Migrants and settlers

Many of the movements described above were of field workers to plantation economies and peasants to industrial economies in the nineteenth century, and labouring and service workers to rich economies in the twentieth. Not all movements follow the poor-to-rich pattern; some indeed follow a rich-to-rich route, such as movements of people from European countries to the USA, Canada and Australia. And not all migrations are destined for poorly- or lower-paid work in the new country. Movement of professionals – commonly in English referred to as a 'brain drain' – sees doctors, engineers, accountants, teachers, academics and researchers, information technologists, moving from Third World to First World destinations (Indian and African doctors to Britain, Indian software specialists to the USA and Germany), from former Soviet and East European countries to Western societies (Russian scientists to America), and from First World to First World (British researchers to the USA). Typically the countries of origin bear some or all of the social cost of 'producing' these professionals even though the final leg of training may be in the destination country. About 12 per cent of all academic staff in UK universities were born outside the UK (Fenton, Carter and Modood 2000).

Countries which are difficult to enter can become notably open when specific skill shortages are identified. Thus both Germany and the USA have targeted Indian-trained information technology workers where Indian education in mathematics and technology continues to be of a high order. Indian workers are well paid in America by comparison with their potential earnings in India. But in their absence American employers would have to pay much more for home-trained staff. This is not only because home staff would demand and expect more, but also because in the absence of Indian 'competitors' their market situation would be much stronger. The National Health Service in Britain has had to adopt a concerted strategy for the importation of trained nursing staff from both European and other sources.

There are other features of labour migration, professional or labouring, which are variable and important. Two in particular are legality and permanence. For all the legal migrant workers in the world there are millions of illegals; for all the workers with appropriate papers, there are millions of 'undocumented' workers (Castles 2000). Legality is a singularly crucial question, since illegal workers and those who fear that their legality as migrants may be brought into question are unable to act as full citizens of their new country, and unable even to attempt to use the protections that may be open to them. With respect to what we have said about people being able to rely on the state, or the rule of law, to protect them – or at least to have a reasonable hope that it might – undocumented workers, even though living in stable states, have no state to call upon for protection. In addition, the question of legality goes much further than the illegal workers themselves. In a society where, for example, the right to stay and the right to bring in spouses and dependants, and the right to leave and return, are constantly in question for those without proper documents, these rights may become questioned and 'questionable' for all those from the same origin as the 'illegals'. The uncertainty and anxiety on the one hand (among migrant families) and the suspiciousness and aggression on the other (among public authorities, immigration officers) become 'generalized' well beyond those who may actually have made an illegal entry. This set of expectations, suspicions, apprehension and caution penetrate the choices taken both by migrants themselves and by police and immigration officers.

It should not be imagined that receiving societies unqualifiedly deplore illegal immigrants. In public they do, and 'ordinary citizens' – as against politicians – frequently join in the condemnation of illegals and the 'threat' they pose to the integrity of the receiving society. But there can be little doubt that the destination societies frequently will tacitly condone the arrival of illegals simply because they constitute necessary labour which can scarcely be recruited from any other source. Undocumented workers have advantages over legally settled workers from the point of view of the state and of employers. If migrant workers generally are liable to exploitation, undocumented workers are liable to super-exploitation since it takes only one false move for them to be removed by their employer or threatened with exposure. Equally, if migrant workers calculate the acceptability of their earnings in part by comparing them with expectations in their home countries, then undocumented migrant workers are likely to accept even lower income and dirty or dangerous work. The numbers of illegal immigrant workers in, for example, the USA and Malaysia (from, respectively, Mexico and Indonesia, poorer neighbours with land borders) constitute necessary labour in fruit-picking and oil-palm plantations; it is difficult to imagine that the two states receiving these workers have exhausted their talent for keeping out or rooting out 'illegals'. On the other hand a steady or intermittent campaign against them, which does not drive them all away, functions to maintain the climate of insecurity whilst continuing to benefit from the labour of these workers. Malaysia, for example, has stated that it needs a population roughly double its current size if it is to have the human resources to meet the needs of a modernizing economy. This raises the question of how Malaysia would be placed if it were to remove tens of thousands of illegal Indonesian plantation and construction workers (*Guardian*, 16 August 2002) as well as the illegal Indonesian maids whose work enables Malaysian women to join the labour force.

The second feature noted above is permanence. People behave quite differently when they know that they are entering or are engaged in a relationship which is expected to endure than when some engagement is merely fleeting. This is true of all parties to the exchanges or investments in trust that are made. Many migrants leave their home country with an expectation of return, the more so in the modern period when travel is fast and easy – the less so when highlanders left the west of Scotland by boat in the nineteenth century. The overwhelming majority of migrants from the Caribbean to Britain in the 1950s expected to return home after a few years, as did many Italian migrants to America. The disputed sociological interpretations of the housing choices of Pakistani migrants to Britain partly turned on whether they expected to stay (Rex and Moore 1967; Dahya 1974). If they intended to return to Pakistan they would see their housing in Britain as a temporary expedient; if they were to stay in Britain it would become an investment. In situations like this migrants often stay despite their intentions to return – hence what has so often been referred to as the 'myth of return'. The factors favouring a decision to stay begin to mount quite high: if there are children they will soon be mid-education; the migrant generation may see few opportunities for returning; they may also have heard from some who have returned that home has irrevocably changed since they were last there, usually making it seem less attractive. Changes in immigration laws and procedures may also incline people to stay where they are: if they choose to go home they might not get back in should they find 'home' unattractive.

Ethnicity, minority and majority

Migration and the definition of migrant workers and their families as 'ethnic' is a very important topic for those interested in 'ethnicity', or the social mobilization of culture and descent. Many of the populations identified as 'ethnic' in the contemporary world are identified as such because they are viewed by an indigenous population as in-comers, whether their migration is relatively recent or quite distant. In the first and second generation of settlement in-migrating communities may be subjected to labels and titles which they do not choose, both polite and less polite. In Britain 'in-comers' who arrived in the 1950s and 1960s constituted a generation who have since had children, grandchildren, and great-grandchildren born in Britain. The population of migrants and descendants as a whole is, nonetheless, liable to be referred to by some people as 'immigrants'.

After a generation or two, people with parents from the sub-continent of India and from the Caribbean began to exert some influence, if not control, over the terms that were publicly used. On the one hand there was a drive for solidarity of a whole population who were likely to experience racial hostility. This was the attempt to consolidate a politically black identity. There was also a push towards the recognition of diversity and differences which were obscured or ignored both by the political 'black' label and by the generalizing terms – 'black', 'Asian' – used by British media and academics (cf. Modood 1992).

In the case of Indians in Fiji and Malaysia, they remain identified as non-indigenous even though they have had a presence in their respective countries for a century or more. This persistence of the status as 'in-comers' or 'immigrants' well beyond the migration period can be found all over the world and is the basis of the definition of an ethnic community. The idea of 'descent' is largely bound up with the identification of a country of origin even though this may, and often does, entirely neglect social differences among the in-migrant population. So for example 'Italian Americans' is a new category in a new situation and may ignore internal distinctions between, say, Sicilians and other regional groups. Some aspects of cultural difference, such as food, are partly retained, partly modified and taken up by non-Italians; others, such as language, decline.

Although this question of the maintenance of cultural difference was always the primary one in a long-standing sociological interest (Yinger 1994; Gordon 1964), described as the study of 'adaptation', 'acculturation' and 'assimilation', sociologists would now recognize that this is not the primary question however important it remains (Alba 2000). At least it is not the primary question in the way that it has conventionally been posed. There are a number of reasons for this. One is that there is a recognition that changes in customary practice, the use of language, the sustaining of religious faith and affiliation and the enforcement of marriage and kinship rules, are not bound to be exclusively shifts in a single direction, that is the direction of likeness to a dominant model of the majority. Second, there is a recognition that changes in custom and culture, including 'acculturative' changes, do not necessarily imply the disappearance of the collective identity. In the case of the USA there seems to be some recognition of the fact that collective identities have persisted despite the widespread pattern of 'Americanization'.

This is the case where acculturation has occurred but identities persist. Gans has referred to this as 'symbolic ethnicity' (Gans 1979, 1994; see discussion in previous chapter).

Third, it remains necessary to sustain a distinction between what *individuals* do (with respect to their ethnic identity) and whether and how a *collective* identity persists. Put rather simply, American Jewishness can persist as can a group called 'American Jews' or 'Jewish Americans' even if tens of thousands of American Jews abandon Jewishness or cease to be, in any meaningful sense, 'Jews'. There remains also the question of whether individuals in the population described 'act as Jews', that is to say, are oriented to their ethnic identity in choosing how to act. And finally the definition of the identities is not fixed, nor are the cultural forms which are taken to be significant in marking off collectivities. As Barth argued, the cultural items which are taken to be indicative of the assertion of difference and the maintenance of boundaries are particular items 'selected' from a wide range of possible indices of differences; the selection may change. This would be true of the cultural items which are identified by group members *and* those which are made significant by others, non-members. In the early days of Pakistani settlement in the United Kingdom, food and dress were seized on by non-Pakistanis as the marks of difference. Later, Islamic faith and practice was taken to be a leading mark of difference, often emphasized by both members and non-members, especially during and after the Salman Rushdie affair, when Muslims protested against Rushdie's book *The Satanic Verses* (Samad 1992).

In these ways migrant communities and their descendants are a commonplace foundation of the organization of ethnic difference. But the sociology of ethnicity is not synonymous with the sociology of migration. This is not just because there are other forms or foundations of ethnic and ethno-national identities, such as those of oppressed indigenous peoples and non-majority nations or ethno-nations, but also because the sociology of ethnicity is primarily interested in the way ethnic identities and obligations are socially and politically organized, and not necessarily in migration as the primary focus.

The social and political organization
of ethnicity

Two examples will help to illustrate what could be meant by 'the social and political organization of ethnicity'. Both examples turn upon the fact that although family and, more broadly, kinship obligations cannot be equated with ethnicity, nevertheless orientations to the family constitute a kind of 'daily practice' wherein many of the dramas relevant to ethnic identity are acted out. So the first thing to recognize is that migration is in several respects an individualizing enterprise. In many instances, with the very clear exception of political refugees, the underlying motive for migration is personal and family betterment. Migrants will accept that there are many losses as well as gains, chief among the former being the difficulty of maintaining familiar patterns of living, the distance between family members, and the racism encountered in the new country. In some degree the migrant generation knows that these losses are likely to accompany migration, although many 'Commonwealth immigrants' to Britain were taken aback by the strength of racist attitudes and behaviour.

But the migrants may *not* entirely anticipate the extent to which individuation is allied to the search for successful careers and advancement. Although migrants may share *collectively* a goal of improvement or economic 'betterment', the pursuit of an individual or personal path of self-advancement is an individualistic life-aim which is, in the end, contrary to the idea of family solidarity and even ethnic solidarity. Tensions within migrant or former migrant families, *and* within non-migrant families, frequently surround not so much whether individuals can pursue life-aims at the expense of family solidarity, but *how* this tension is managed and how far detachment might go. Precisely the same kind of mobility–loyalty problem is worked out in indigenous working-class families where individuals might 'succeed' (highly approved) and 'forget where they came from' (not approved) (Roberts 1990). *In migrant-origin families all over the world this same tension is likely to be expressed in an ethnic idiom.* In addition to this ethnic version of the problem of individuation, there are usually class divisions within a 'community' defined as ethnic. So when a group is low in status as an ethnic group – on account of the ethnic hierarchies and racist valuations by the majority – it is possible that the successful individual may be seen as guilty of a double betrayal, betrayal of class and betrayal of people. More precisely, betrayal of class may be *viewed as* betrayal of people.

The second illustration turns more particularly on individuation and the position of women in the family, in work and career life, and in the cultivation of ethnic difference. This is a special case and extension of the above problem of individuation, with the added dimension of gender and ethnicity. No set of sociological theorems will match all cases. There are many migrations which are led by women, as in the case of maids and nurses recruited from poor to rich countries. But where migrations are 'led' by men there is frequently some disruption of 'traditional' values and practices. Men may break with custom by linking up with women who are not co-ethnics; they may certainly abandon, albeit temporarily, restraints in dress, religious observance and daily practice. Punjabi men in Britain stopped wearing turbans in order to get jobs (Ballard and Ballard 1977; Ballard 1994). Changes in custom may also be because of the absence of women who, if present, would have had a role in the enforcing of family and ethnic custom. Women can be important in the business of enforcing custom. They teach language to their children, play a key role in the planning of family business, often take the lead in 'connecting' – keeping up obligations to others, remembering birthdays and other family celebrations, and in some sense 'controlling' men. Women are also critically implicated in custom itself as, for example, the main focus of marriage arrangements; what are sometimes regarded as traditional attitudes and practice are frequently rules about gender roles and the proper behaviour of women (see Anthias and Yuval-Davis 1992; Bradley 1996; Shaw 1988).

These tensions are implicit both within the histories of migration and in the formation and reformation of ethnic identities and communities (Jacobson 1997a, 1997b). The tension is between the solidarity which is the ideal of family, extended family and ethnic community life, and the individuation and individualism which is implicated in 'success' and mobility in the new environment, a tension which is particularly acute for women. That is, women whose family origins are in what come to be termed 'traditional communities' face not only resistance to mobility from a majority population with a command of the social and cultural capital essential to inclusion, but also resistance from within their communities of origin where the 'liberation' – i.e. individuation and individualism – of women is seen as especially a breach with traditional values. Thus women of minority ethnic groups take the lead in fighting racism and discrimination coming from outside their community and patriarchy coming from within it (*Guardian*, 14 August 2001). It is therefore not surprising that these women find majority women (in rich Western societies such as the UK and the USA, typically white women) advancing a kind of feminism which is out of tune with or unsympathetic to the dilemmas and interests of minority women (Mirza 1997). Similarly, minority women have two difficult priorities which are hard to reconcile: recognizing and opposing the racism and discrimination that they and their ethnic brothers experience, whilst opposing their ethnic brothers in the matter of 'traditional' attitudes to women.

Mobility and resistance

A great deal has been written about so-called ethnic minority groups, in particular with regard to two principal things. One is determining the nature of the racism that they experience; the second is how to account for racism, what its source is. The further back one goes the more likely it is that the term 'racism' has the narrower association with beliefs in a racial hierarchy and in inherent inequality. The hierarchy of races is identified above all by physical and visible differences, and popular ideas come close to matching the nineteenth- and twentieth-century would-be science of the races of humankind. Such views always had their utterly malign and apparently benign and paternalist versions; rather than 'racism', they may be captured by the phrase 'white supremacy' with its overt expression in pre-1950s USA or South Africa (Cell 1982; Fredrickson 1972, 1988). The postwar British Cabinets expressed frankly racist views of this kind ('keep Britain white') when Commonwealth immigration was discussed, largely in private (Carter, Harris and Joshi 1987; Rattansi 2002). But this conception of racism has proved far from adequate to covering all the forms of social exclusion, gatekeeper discriminations, maintaining of social distance, the valuation of culture difference, ethnic patterns of social inequality, and outright hatred and violence. It is clear that something more complex is at work than the 'mere' application of a doctrine of racial difference and inequality.

The answer has been to invent a multitude of racisms – institutional, cultural and societal are examples – with the result not only that the term loses all precision, but that it is also seen as description, diagnosis and explanation at one sweep (Miles 1993). The word seems destined to retain this broad and diffuse all-embracing meaning in public discourse which means that public debates become rather confused and confusing. However, there is usually something in the public discourse which is undeniable, widespread and important: that is, some sense of profound rejection of or antagonism towards visible minorities, coupled with a resistance to hearing their voice, and occasionally accompanied by the most appalling acts of violence not only by particular private individuals but also by agents of the state, the police and the penal system.

In a racist climate, acts of violence, social exclusions and unequal treatment occur on a daily basis (Virdee 1995). But we also need to be much more particular about specific contexts, about different racisms, and about explanatory frames which can be quite diverse. Wieviorka has made a start on this by developing a distinction between differentialist and inequalitarian racisms. In the first the principal impulse is to establish the utter 'otherness' of an excluded, despised or oppressed group (Wieviorka 1995). Thus the other group is not only culturally different but is also in some sense 'beyond understanding' or 'beyond acceptance or acceptability' in its profound otherness. In the second the impulse is to keep the others 'in their proper place', in inferior positions, at the service of a dominant class or ethnie, and to reinforce their status as less worthy and less deserving of full or equal incorporation.

The former (differentialist) might be expressed by the majority German posture towards Jews in Nazi Germany and the latter (inequalitarian) by the white American posture towards black Americans. Differentialist racism can incline towards obliteration of 'the other' since they are seen as so profoundly different and their presence may be represented as impure and polluting. In inequalitarian racism the impulse is not so much to obliterate them as to exploit 'them', or to sustain a social superiority over the other. As Wieviorka himself observes, this is a useful but not always sustainable distinction. But it does illustrate how there is not a single tangible, definitively limited thing called 'racism' to which we can attribute multifold causal power. Rather there are a number of contexts, relationships and situations of power and dominance in which 'others' are represented as inherently different or lesser and these representations become defining elements of the relationships. This idea of 'inherent difference' may be expressed as different by nature (i.e. 'typical of them', racially conceived) or different by culture where culture is viewed as a fixed attribute ('that's what they do', 'that's what they are like').

Thus for example in the early period of the settlement of black Caribbean and South Asian people in Britain, much of the early expression of racism surrounded health and disease, social contact and housing (Solomos 1993; Layton-Henry 1984). Migrants were associated with tubercular infection; dance halls were either to be places where white women might associate with black men or were places where controversial 'colour bars' were applied; and many of the early disputes about the arrival of immigrants were linked with housing. Subsequently the health scares diminished in significance, colour bars in public premises were outlawed, and schooling and employment began to assume greater significance. Furthermore the centre of attention has shifted from an immigrant generation to their children and grandchildren, who are bound to be affronted by an implication that they have fewer rights or lesser entitlement than others to social goods and rewards. Therefore by the new century (twenty-first) the question of *racism in Britain* has two primary manifestations: one is with respect to social mobility, equal opportunities and incorporation, the second is with regard to national identity and the response provoked from (some segments of) the majority by the new politics of multiculturalism, ethnicity and identity.

We shall turn to the second modality of racism – the national identity question – a little bit later. But it is the mobility agenda which concerns us here, because it is the agenda which is simultaneously a source of collective action – mobilization against racism and discrimination – and a mode of individuation, that is the mobility of and incorporation of the individual which may be at the expense of collective ties and sentiments. In other words, one response to racism and discrimination is, in effect, a universalist response, that of extending and perfecting the equal opportunities and meritocratic agenda. Social mobility is not *necessarily* a solvent of ethnic identities since people may retain a broad identification with a 'descent and culture community' even when class differentiation becomes more and more elaborated. Evidently ethnic identities do not depend on a shared class base. On the other hand much of the shared experience of urban migrants *is* a class experience and the greater the social mobility and class differentiation within an urban migrant (and their descendants) community the more this base of shared experience is eroded. We can be sure that for governments and policy-makers in multi-ethnic societies, breaking a link between class (disadvantage) and ethnic identity is an important strategy, even if difficult to achieve. Thus in Britain, in the new millennium, advocates of 'diversity' and 'multi-ethnicity' can be recruited to the New Labour Party's stress on 'modernization' and to an equal opportunities ideology which stresses meritocracy rather than redistribution.

This ethnicity–mobility strategy, pursued both by governments and by community leaders, is only partially successful and for a number of reasons. One is that when incoming people are defined by (many of) the majority as both ethnically different and as less entitled, or not entitled at all, to advancements and resources (of health care, housing and education), resistance will be mounted at all junctures. In the early days of Caribbean and South Asian immigration to Britain there were many signs of attempts to confine 'coloured' migrants to a narrow band of employment and housing opportunities (Smith 1989; C. Brown 1984; Miles 1993; Brown and Gay 1985). Movement out of those sectors, or promotion within them, was made extremely difficult by an often-hidden subversion of mobility for immigrants and subsequently their children. Later generations began to compete in entirely new areas of employment – in clerical, administrative and public service occupations, the service industries, and the professional sectors – and in virtually all of these sectors a pattern of resistance or only partial incorporation has been reported (Fenton, Carter and Modood 2000). This is the pattern which has come to be described as 'institutional racism'. Some manifestations may be violent and abusive. But in large organizations its core is a pattern of tacit resistance to the mobility of 'minorities'.

It is not to be imagined that ethnic identities and the persistence of communal boundaries are wholly or even mainly a function of the actions of a powerful 'other'. This would be to reduce ethnic identities to a kind of 'reactive' status whereby people 'A' are seen to cling to their identity as 'A's because the 'B's treat them poorly or refuse to admit them fully to 'B' society. Clearly people in some measure control their own identity and make their own choices about life partners, marriage partners, circles of affiliation, careers, religious observance and their children's education – all things which may influence or be part of the sustaining of ethnic boundaries. But these choices are not made in a vacuum, in the autonomous space of an ethnic group. They are made partly in response to, or as a mode of relating to, 'others' who play a part in patrolling the borders between groups. Thus racism in its broadest usage, as a series of acts of violence, stereotyping, social exclusions, public and private abuse and defamations, and tacit practices of disregard, must have a part in the sustaining of ethnic boundaries (Jenkins 1997). To call it all racism is to look for a single (and rather ill-defined) cause of some rather different social processes. This multitude of acts of 'tacit resistance to the mobility of minorities' experienced in sometimes dramatic and sometimes wholly mundane ways by 'ethnically other' teachers, students,

134 Migration, Ethnicity and Mobilization

schoolchildren, nurses, doctors, shop assistants and cus-
tomers, factory workers, journalists, neighbours, and sports
players and watchers, is a significant part of the replication
of ethnic boundaries in everyday life. These partial exclusions
and open or hidden injuries of ethnic antagonisms may
prompt a collective and communalist response in ethnic
mobilization and the politics of cultural and communal
recognition.

Summary

In the early part of this chapter we discussed the circumstances in which social and cultural difference becomes the
basis – in a new context – of ethnic identity. Of all these contexts we focused on migration. Most observers note not only
that world migration has increased in scope and scale since
the 1960s, but also that it will continue to grow and affect
most countries of the world. It seems certain that this will be
the basis of new 'ethnicity situations', where migrant groups
see themselves or are seen by others as different in important
respects. But ethnicity is not only about difference. In so
many instances throughout the world, cultural difference is
associated with unequal social relations. It is not simply, in
Barth's language, a matter of sustaining boundaries between
groups, but also of sustaining inequalities of power and
access to social resources.

7
Conditions of Ethnicity: Global Economy and Precarious States

In the previous chapter we referred to the massive movement of population to the United States from Europe in the nineteenth century. These movements were conditioned by grand-scale economic changes, in particular the failure of peasant economies in Europe and the availability of land plus the energetic growth of capitalist industrialism in the United States. Thus we illustrated how international migration creates the circumstances for ethnic identity formation. In the present chapter we shall look at three further, and more abstractly conceived, sets of conditions which influence the formation of ethnic differentiation. These conditions are the terms under which actors choose to act in accordance with an ethnic identification.

These conditions of action are conceived here as: (1) the global and local implications of gross economic inequalities, (2) the degree of security which a state is able to guarantee to its citizens, that is the greater or lesser 'precariousness' of the state, and (3) the influence on state politics, including ethnic politics, of inter-state politics and geo-political changes. In the present and the recent past, the collapse of the communist world is the most significant geo-political change.

Theorizing the conditions of ethnic action

The development of a unitary theory of 'ethnicity' is a mirage, as is the search for an ultimately precise definition of ethnicity or ethnic groups. However enticing the word 'ethnicity' may be – and it appears to have trapped any number of writers in its web – it is mainly a descriptor for a broad field of interest. Of itself it has no precise point of reference, of itself it has no explanatory power. As I argued before (Fenton 1999) the *variants* or 'forms' of 'ethnic groups' are at least as significant as the common ground between them, and the *contexts* in which they may be found are the source of explanation rather than any inherent qualities of ethnicity itself. In order to understand the struggles of Australian Aboriginal peoples we need to know something about 'indigenousness' as a political principle and as the basis of a movement and its particular manifestation in Australian history (being the particular case); and we need to know a great deal about land, colonial dispossession, economic growth in Australia, state power and the colonial formation of the Australian state (being the historical context). If we also draw on a theorization of how groups mobilize, guard their boundaries, and state their claims of both an instrumental and a symbolic kind, we are applying sociological theorems both to the case and to the context.

In chapter 6 I described a framework, following Eriksen (Eriksen 1993; Fenton 1999), for identifying different types of (more or less) mobilized groups which could be and are described as 'ethnic'. The second task was to set out a series of historical trajectories within which these groups or collective identities had taken shape; slavery, the colonial social order, world migrations, and the unfinished business of nation-formation. These are the contexts which give rise to ethnic identities and politics. They are also the parameters within which people choose to, are compelled to or are induced to act in accordance with ethnic identities. It is this last task to which I wish to return. I intend to sketch out a theory of global and societal change as the backdrop to cultural movements, political mobilizations, and collective identities which are commonly described as ethnic, and equally frequently as 'nationalist' and 'racist'. We cannot attempt a totalizing or global sociology here but we can establish some outlines of those principal features of the contemporary world which are most effective in the determination of the phenomena we call 'ethnic'.

Features of the contemporary world

Inequalities of a grand scale between the richest and poorest zones of the world remain a feature of the contemporary global economy, a feature which has shown no sign of diminishing since the immediate post-colonial period of the 1960s. Almost certainly these inequalities have increased not only because material poverty of an absolute kind, coupled with near poverty and chronic insecurity, continues in the poorest zones, but also because the enrichment of a minority reaches ever new heights. These inequalities can be identified by citing nation-states in a simple listing of the poorest and the richest countries – from the USA, Germany and Japan to Chad, Bangladesh and Burkina Faso. But a more accurate account separates the global rich from the global poor in a way that both identifies rich and poor zones and states but also identifies rich and poor classes within them. The most persuasive and concise account of this formation is to be found in Ankie Hoogvelt's 'Globalisation and the Postcolonial World' (2000; see also Hirst and Thompson 1999), whose writing is the basis of what follows.

Hoogvelt establishes first of all that 'Economic, social and power relations have been recast to resemble not a pyramid but a three tier structure of concentric circles. All three circles cut across national and regional boundaries.' She then goes on to define the three concentric circles thus:

1 The elites of all continents and nations, albeit in different proportions in relation to their respective geographic hinterlands . . . (this is some 20 per cent of the world's population who are 'bankable').
2 The above are encircled by a fluid larger social layer of between 20 and 30 per cent of the world population

(workers and their families) who labour in insecure forms of employment, thrown into cut-throat competition in the global market.

3 The third and largest, concentric circle comprises those who are already effectively excluded from the global system. Performing neither a productive function, nor presenting a potential consumer market in the present stage of high tech information-driven capitalism, there is for the moment neither theory, world view, nor moral injunction to include them in universal progress.

These are not just classifications of groups. They are held together by arguments about how the global system works. The secret of the first group is to be found in the phrase 'bankable'. That is to say they do not simply have 'more' than the others – more yachts, more world travel, more money, more accommodation – but they are able to convert this surplus into social leverage and economic power. With respect to the second they are chronically vulnerable to the effects of new technologies and the decisions made by corporate managers and political leaders. In Hoogvelt's words, 'State of the art technology, frenzied capital mobility and neo-liberal policies together ensure both a relentless elimination of jobs by machines, and a driving down of wages and conditions to the lowest global denominator' (p. 358).

For the third group development has virtually passed them by and for them the future promises 'containment and exclusion'. There is here, then, not just a classification of the rich, middle and poor, but a theoretical account of world capitalism in which corporate capital and the organized pursuit of profit produces a rich class which manages, a labouring class which produces a surplus for minimum rewards, and an excluded poor for whom global capitalism offers virtually nothing beyond the merest survival, and frequently not even that.

Much of this is grounded in well-established political economy, but with an emphasis on the global economy rather than the nation-state. The *divergence* from political economy (as understood in the 1960s and 1970s) comes in our contemporary understanding of *the political consequences* of this formation. In this respect the world has, as ever, moved faster than social theory. The principal changes from the immediate post-colonial period are the decline of optimism about 'development' especially with regard to Africa, the intensification of exclusion and poverty, the inclusion of some East Asian economies into the global system, the demise of the state communist project and the Soviet empire, the weakening or abandonment of socialist and welfarist politics in rich Western states, and the spreading of neo-liberal politics in rich, poor and formerly state communist societies.

These kinds of social changes are typically understood as 'structural' in that they constitute the external forms of economic organization and the disposition of power. Only with enormous effort can the acts of individuals, even when organized collectively, surmount these structures, as was illustrated by Cesar Chavez and the thousands of super-exploited Mexican field workers in California in the 1970s. But the power of this 'external structure' does not indicate a theory which denies the agency of individuals who live within it. Indeed the effects of these global movements penetrate into the daily lives of people all over the world in the most mundane and immediate senses. This might be in people's ability to purchase the transport which would lead them to employment, their ability to hold on to meagre allotments of land upon which their livelihood depends, their ability to purchase a home, afford education, and keep their families, in even the most modest way, secure, intact and whole. In other words this global 'structure' constitutes the stage on which at the micro-social level people make decisions about how to sustain a tolerable life, how to improve their prospects, how to resist their displacement and dispossession, about what they regard as valuable and about whom to trust.

The choices made by those with economic and state power provoke a response in the choices made by less powerful actors. This second set of choices – to organize, to labour uncomplainingly, to withdraw, to resist, to circumvent the law in search of gain, to migrate legally and illegally, to promote the messages of their religious faith or of their culture and descent community – these choices too provoke a response in a second set of choices made by powerful and influential actors. There is, then, no endless mystery of structure and agency. Each of these sets of choices produces tem-

porary situations, which are materially and culturally constituted. In Hoogvelt's terms, these are 'post-colonial conditions', or different relationships to the world economy. The
main character of these situations *is not ethnic* – but in virtually every one we can detect the outlines of action, organization and cultural innovation which have some of the
features of ethnicity.

Post-colonial economic conditions

Hoogvelt indicates that she uses the term 'post-colonial' in
order to 'capture the notion that the distinct social formations which have emerged are a result of the way in which
the aftermath of colonialism interacts with the forces of globalisation' (2000, p. 359). The first of these post-colonial conditions is 'exclusion and anarchy' which is 'exemplified in
sub-Saharan Africa, where the patrimonial state form emerging after independence proved too weak to weld a viable
political unity or civil society out of the mosaic of ethnic fragments bequeathed by colonial administrations'. The second
is the 'anti-developmentalism of Islam' where 'the failure of
the developmentalist project, coupled with the exclusionary
effect of . . . globalisation, has interacted with the spirit of
renewal ever-present within Islam *and* with its long history
of confrontation with the West'. The third, typically in East
Asia, is where 'the state-led developmentalist project has suc-
ceeded in catapulting the economies of a small number of
NICs [newly industrialized countries] into the heartland of
the reconstructed global capitalist system'. The fourth is typified by the South American 'revolt against Western models of
modernity and progress' whilst being a 'testing ground for
neo-liberal policies of globalisation and privatisation'.

The situations which Hoogvelt here describes virtually correspond to poorer zones of the global economy – sub-Saharan
Africa, (some) Islamic countries, South America, plus the new
entrant to international capitalist success, East Asia. But the
divisions between 'the bankable', 'the insecure but employed
labouring classes' and the 'excluded' population can also be
applied *within* each region or state. Thus the socially and eco-

nomically excluded of the USA's vast degraded urban spaces, America's white, black and Hispanic poor, belong either to the excluded and impoverished population or at best to the insecurely employed, perpetually at the mercy of shifts in markets, downsizings, relocations and vast and rapid movements of capital and points of production. These economic insecurities are *in principle* ethnic-blind. International corporations are interested in exploiting workers, not just white or black workers. But the political and social responses in a society with a historic racialized discourse are themselves highly racialized.

W. J. Wilson and the disappearance of work

No one has done more to explain and demystify this situation in the United States than William Julius Wilson. He first argued that the social disadvantages of an excluded African American population could not be fully explained by reference to the racialized attitudes of whites. He followed this with an equally compelling analysis of the 'disappearance of work' (Wilson 1999).

It is crucial to Wilson's thesis that not only are African Americans subject to disproportionate exclusion from paid employment but also that many white Americans are similarly excluded or, if in work, live in a more or less permanent state of anxiety about its continuation. In this situation (some) white political responses do not reproduce the categorical racism of an earlier period, but do give voice to a new racism which associates black people with welfare, crime and fecklessness. This is coupled with a populist and racist politics which is opposed to welfare spending especially where this is seen to benefit an 'undeserving' and racialized population. This means that there is a powerful momentum behind a kind of anti-welfarist politics thus obstructing those modest ameliorations which state-funded interventions might bring both to identified ethnic minorities (such as affirmative actions) and to all the disadvantaged (measures to protect employment, improve education, and social security). This politicization of ethnic difference takes place against a backdrop of massive increases in joblessness. Speaking of three neighbourhoods representing the 'historic core of the Black Belt in the city of Chicago' he writes:

In 1950 69 per cent of all males aged fourteen and over who lived in these neighborhoods worked in a typical week, and in 1960, 64 per cent of this group were so employed. However by 1990 only 37 per cent of all males aged sixteen and over held jobs in a typical week in these three neighborhoods. (Wilson 1999, p. 480)

This pattern of joblessness is caused or exacerbated by movements within the global economy. Employment in the United States is 'exported' when American capital in, for example, the computer microchip and processor industry relocates to Central America or South East Asia to take advantage of lower wage costs and lighter regulation. Employment in America is undermined when goods are imported (e.g. in clothes) which take the place of American employment in the same product area (Wilson 1999).

Elijah Anderson has made similar arguments in his contribution to the retrospective review of *Beyond the Melting Pot*. He suggests that Glazer and Moynihan overestimated the likely social and economic assimilation of African Americans. This could partly have been because they underestimated the strength of racist ideologies in the USA. But, writes Anderson, 'Glazer and Moynihan could not have anticipated changes in the economic structure and in immigration'. Part of this economic change is to be found in the de-industrialization of the USA:

Today, we are experiencing the transformation of American cities from centers of manufacturing to centers of service and high technology. The loss of well-paying manufacturing jobs in the cities as U.S. corporations have sent their low-skill jobs to Third World countries and non-metropolitan areas of this country has devastated the black working class. (E. Anderson 2000, p. 267)

These patterns are by no means confined to the United States. And they are patterns which frequently follow ethnic contours of the population. In most rich multi-ethnic societies we find examples of ethnic mobilization, and of the ethnic politics of redistribution and recognition. These are typically accompanied by a reactionary politics of 'race' or ethnicity among majority ethnic groups, and by a racialized or 'ethnicized' discourse in the politics of immigration, welfare and crime. This would be true of most of Western Europe, the USA, and of Australia and Canada in all of which countries or regions there is a demographic and tacit cultural white European majority. As we saw in chapter 1, however, the historical circumstances of the USA have bestowed upon it a peculiar formulation of a post-slavery black–white bimodality.

The difficulties of minority ethnic groups in rich societies are frequently economic in the way in which we have described; they are also likely to be broadly political in the reactionary politics of 'race and racism'. The white poor and disaffected are one group who are likely to interpret their own disadvantages as somehow caused by 'racial others', what Wieviorka (1995) has termed the 'poor white mentality'. In the rich 'First World' countries there is not a 'generalized' breakdown of state functions but, nonetheless, minority groups may not only lack for protection by the state, they may also be victims of state action itself. This is true for minorities in rich societies such as African Americans and Australian Aboriginal peoples, for Roma in the Czech republic (Guy 2001), and many other cases where people cannot rely on just treatment by the police or state administration. This can be contrasted with instances where there is a *generalized* breakdown of state functions and (sometimes) a state dominated by a particular ethnic elite.

Precarious states

The authority of the state, and its failures, can be and often are decisive in the determination of group conflict. In sub-Saharan Africa 'the patrimonial state form emerging after independence proved too weak' to create a stable polity or support a functioning civil society in the fragmented post-colonial order. This instability, which is both political and economic, 'overwhelmed the fragile social and political orders' (Hoogvelt 2000). In contemporary France, Michel Wieviorka's arguments support a parallel kind of analysis. He is discussing what he calls 'the crisis of the state and the rise of community' and advances a general proposition:

One or more communal movements may form and become active in situations where several communities, previously combined within a single political unit, have ceased to accept their integration and are demanding either a new deal – a different distribution of power for example – or that the association be dissolved. (Wieviorka 1995)

He discusses in particular the disintegration of the Lebanese state in the 1970s as an example of a case where 'the determining factor might be a crisis of the state which had, up to that point, been capable of managing the pluri-communal society'. As the state structure collapsed

the action and . . . the violence seem to be a product, among other factors, not of purely defensive behaviours or nationalist ideologies, *but of deficiencies on the part of the state which open up a space for confrontations in which each community* . . . defends its territories and yet seeks also to exert influence on the political life of the country, the region and even, in some cases, the whole world. (Wieviorka 1995, p. 111; my emphasis)

The deficiencies of state authority in impoverished societies have a profound influence on the choices people make about whom they can trust. This in turn is implicated by the importance which people attach to – and may *have* to attach to – alliances based on kin.

I have argued elsewhere that it is possible to reverse the emphasis of Geertz when he suggests that states may have difficulty establishing their 'writ' against the primordial allegiances of regional, religious, linguistic and ethnic groups. The 'other way round' would be to suggest that ethnic allegiances become and remain important – possibly all-important – in states which have failed to secure power and loyalty throughout their territory and through all or most institutional arenas (Fenton 1999). This links together kinship, ethnicity and the state in a single theoretical argument. In her analysis of Somalia Simons adds a fourth dimension, democracy, thus linking together kinship, ethnic loyalty, state power and the ability to sustain democratic institutions (Simons 1997).

Whom can you trust?

It is worth inspecting Simons' paper in some considerable detail not only because it is an instructive case study, but because it is instructive *across* a series of concepts and theorizations of ethnicity. To put it in context the paper is a discussion of conflict in Somalia, the limited power of the state, and the dangers of trying to implement democracy when individuals do not have material or personal security and cannot be guaranteed security and freedom of action. Corresponding to the rather broad distinction between kin and non-kin societies she sees democracy as workable only when 'individuation' has progressed to a stage where individuals are free to act and to 'identify' independently. By 'individuation' here, Simons means the extent to which any individual is able to pursue a course of action which is dissociated from any group (kin, ethnic group, and so on) that is liable to make a claim on the individual. When the state guarantees security (personal security, some measure of economic security, and of welfare and entitlements) individuation is possible: 'What I mean by individuation is that individuals are able to stay apart, construct their own political identities if they so choose, *and deny the claims of others.* In Somalia none of these are options over which individuals have sufficient, or any, control' (Simons 1997, p. 278; my emphasis).

We could reverse this proposition by suggesting that ethnicity is powerful where individuals are unable to deny the claims of others. The Somali state, Simons argues, 'never sufficiently proved itself credible as the guarantor of a secure future to any of its citizens'. Under these circumstances 'traditional ties' are all the more important. Kinship relationships are the focus of what Simons calls 'charts of trustworthiness':

Somalis follow strategies [which are] common among nomadic pastoralists around the world and are grounded in the trust and obligation encoded in genealogical relationships . . . genealogies chart links among kin which are only kept if people prove worth remaining tied to . . . they are charts of trustworthiness. (p. 276)

People depend on kin because they cannot depend on the state. Some networks of kin of course are on the other side of the line – they *are* the state.

Trust societies are contrasted with individuated societies where individuals are able to detach themselves from kin because they can rely on the state. Indeed the state may have actively promoted detachment from kin in order to increase loyalty to the state as well as to achieve other objectives such as universal education or maximum labour mobility. In individuated societies the state 'does tend to be regarded as the guarantor of the future. The state remaining, not becoming, stable is what most citizens count on.' This has a moral dimension so that in trust societies kin are people whom you *must* rely upon and support; in individuated societies *you are expected* to 'go your own way'. In the 'liberated' circumstances individuals not only *can afford* situational identities over which they exercise choice, they *are bound to have* situational identities:

Meanwhile having to be situational also means individuals' identities cannot be unitary. Having to be situational means people have to be allowed to selectively display or hide their multiple allegiances to or from a wide variety of entities: family, party, church, friends, work. Nor are these loyalties automatically (or even) nested. Rather citizens recognise that they can reveal or deny all sorts of affiliations by choice. This is what freedom, for many people, amounts to. (p. 279)

The 'moral compulsion to assist kin' runs quite contrary to this kind of freedom and quite contrary to identities of situation and of choice.

The final part of Simons' argument is that in the absence of these freedoms the institutions of democracy are difficult to sustain since democracy is predicated on the isolated individual able to remain free of other influences, and owing primary civic loyalty to the idea of nation and state (cf. Geertz 1973). Without established and reliably independent state power and with little economic stability or security, the implementation of democracy may yield its opposite – organized conflict between kin or 'ethnic' groups.

These are telling observations about the very nature of ethnic conflict and violence in weak-state societies. Academics typically respond critically to standard press interpretations of such conflicts; where the press suggest that they are the consequence of ancient hatreds, academics counterpose an argument pressing the case for the ruthless leadership of ethnic propagandists – in the case of Yugoslavia, the 'devil Milosevic' as against 'the ancient hatreds' of Croat and Serb. But the academic argument neglects the face-to-face nature of much ethnic violence. It was certainly common in the Yugoslav wars to hear of neighbours killing neighbours whom they had known, happily, for years. Simons argues that ethnic violence is so often based on personal knowledge:

Far too little attention is paid to the fact that often people are killed person by person, quite wilfully and at close quarters. To begin with how does someone even know who should be killed? Presumptions about who should be slain call for some entry into local knowledge. Also wielding hand weapons, even just facing a victim, demands far more personal control than weapons of mass destruction do. . . . This is where the internally consistent logic of mistrusting non-kin (because only kin are trustworthy) ultimately leads – not to senseless destruction but to eminently sensible, pre-emptive, and fairly precise, yet expandable violence. (p. 282)

The phrase 'eminently sensible' may be hard to stomach, but much of the argument is compelling. But if Simons' article were an argument that post-colonial and Third World societies fail to attain the standards needed for 'democracy' then this could rightly be seen as a 'Westernist' understanding, an amalgam of poorly considered ideas, Western arrogance and prejudices towards poorer states. But it is not. Simons' analysis fits entirely with an argument that post-colonial states were in any case frequently ill-designed and hastily established as the West decided that their colonialist projects had run their course. Subsequently they have suffered as a consequence of the unequal conditions of world trade, particularly the devastating effect of world fluctuations in commodity prices coupled with the rising costs of imported manufactured goods (Held and McGrew 2000). There are as a consequence a considerable number of states which can barely pay their way in the world, and could offer neither economic stability nor political security to their citizens. In a number of states – such as Indonesia, the Philippines and Zaire – these conditions have been seriously compounded by corrupt rulers or regimes, often backed by Western powers, which have drained any surplus for their private wealth. In these unstable-economy and weak-state societies (corrupt or not) people cannot afford to forget their relatives. Their relatives on a broader scale become their ethnicity. Thus Simons is quite clear that condemnation of state mismanagement is naive:

by focussing on ways to break the link between economic insolvency and political mismanagement at the top, many writers simply disregard the pressures of lived reality: that if the state (as inherited) is already insolvent, individuals cannot afford to stay separable when genealogy . . . provides a cradle-to-grave civil society. (p. 284)

Poor world to rich world

This account of states and societies typified by economic and state insecurity is enough to suggest that the social conditions of ethnic identities and group loyalties are very different in, say, Somalia compared to the USA. The external co-ordinates of ethnicity in states which lack basic securities are so different from those in rich societies that we can hardly expect ethnic relations to take shape in the same way in both. In some societies the conditions of welfare and security are poor; kin remain important in these conditions in ways which are not matched in rich and relatively stable societies. The frailty or strength of the state as the protector of individuals is not the only decisive variable. Social anthropology as a discipline has taken one of its central tasks to be the understanding of how economic life, land systems and the organization of local decision-making are all implicated in the way individuals are obligated to others in patterns of interdependence and reciprocity (Goddard et al. 1994). This does not mean that people within a particular community or population necessarily like each other; this is not a matter of solidarity and ritual in the purely moral sense. People are bound together 'like it or not' in a way of life which makes them depend on one another. Some of these people are traceable kin, close or distant; others, in a population as large as the Pathans in Pakistan and Afghanistan, simply recognize distant unrelated members as sharing ethnic identity. If the way of life of all, or of a significant proportion of them, is threatened then the sense of interdependency may assert itself ethnically. For the most part this is quite different from the politics of rich industrial and post-industrial societies. What Simons calls the charts of trustworthiness contrast deeply with the individuation of rich 'developed' societies. This question of individuation will, however, merit another look.

This distinction between ethnicity in poor-or-unstable-economy and weak-state societies as against rich and stable economies and established state societies overlaps to a considerable degree with the distinction between societies where the rule of law cannot be relied upon or is not even institutionalized, and those where the rule of law is the established norm and is in theory, but not always in practice, designed to protect all citizens. In the latter type of society the judiciary ought to function independently of the state; the army should be for external defence and not internal control; the police should be impartial in their application of the law so that all citizens can look to them for protection when necessary; ruling groups and individuals should be subject to public review; and the state should function independently of a source of power separate from itself. Typically, when this is not the case, it is a party or army which overwhelms the state or controls central and local affairs in a way such that individuals have no redress. Many people in the world live in societies which lack some or all of the civic conditions just described. Where this is so, the conditions of living, even on a daily basis, may well favour reliance on kin and ethnic identity markers in much the way that Simons has described.

Locating people and trying to play safe

Thus where public safety cannot be guaranteed by an impartial force people must rely on something else. In circumstances of desperation people may claim an ethnic identity other than their own but they will have difficulty making it stick. To illustrate this Simons draws on examples of group identities in Somalia: 'A Darood', she says, 'interrogated by men he suspected of being Hawiye might claim to be from a third group the Hawiye were not targeting. He would not claim to be Hawiye since he could not fake all the connections.' Often, however, a man might not know who his interrogators were. They might 'use a word which only Darood in northeastern Somalia would use, as a signal they too were Darood. If he responded as a Darood he would give himself away. If he did not, and they were Darood, he then risked not being able to convince them that he was too.' Similar kinds of scenes have no doubt been played out in Yugoslavia, Pakistan, Rwanda or Indonesia for example. In some cases differences of appearance, or concentrations in living areas, may make identification relatively simple, but the principle remains the same.

Poverty and economic instability make it all the more difficult for the combination of nation-state obligations and economic interests to succeed in binding individuals into the civic order. To this degree those states which have remained in the poor-economy and weak-state condition for any length of time may come to have a relatively enduring association with ethnic conflict. But this is not a permanent or stable condition – states cannot be classified on an enduring basis in this way because the circumstances of security and uncertainty in both the economy and the polity can change.

Ethnicity and geo-politics

One of the most systematic applications of the principles outlined here, about the relationship between state power, state security and ethnic mobilization, is to be found in Dusko Sekulic's theorization of the dissolution of Yugoslavia (Sekulic 1997). Frequently the starting point for analysis of Yugoslavia in the 1980s and 1990s has been the nature of the communal identities and the history of their antagonisms. The academic response (cf. Bennet 1995; Fenton 1999) has often been to deny the inescapable solidity of ethnic hatreds, and instead to emphasize the relative inter-ethnic harmony of the post Second World War period. The focus then has been on the manipulative nationalist rhetoric of unscrupulous political leaders, usually meaning Milosevic and Tudjman (for a highly detailed historical account the best source is Branka Magas, *The Destruction of Yugoslavia*, 1993; see also Bennet, *Yugoslavia's Bloody Collapse*, 1995). The addition to this framing of the argument, supplied by Sekulic, is to sketch out the dissolution of the state within its *geo-political or geo-strategic context*.

Sekulic begins with an understanding of the state as deriving its legitimacy from its 'external success', grounding this in a Weberian theory of legitimacy. He sees Weber as positing the state as an instrument which can 'hold its own' in the international arena; the creation of and subsequently the legitimation of states commonly reflect a particular historical point of balance between opposing or competing political and military systems.

So in the early part of the twentieth century the creation of a Slav kingdom was an expression of liberation from the Austro-Hungarian empire; Serbian autonomy was already bolstered by the earlier weakening of the Ottoman empire. The stronger position of the Serbs, compared to the Slovenes and Croats, meant that the latter two 'nations' were willing to lose some of their autonomy within a Serb-dominated federation, especially if this helped them protect themselves against encroachments from the north and the west. But despite the fact that Slovenes and Croats gained some protection under the unified kingdom, in the longer run Serb domination meant some curtailment of local rights, for example of the Catholic Croats' freedom of religion, laying the foundations for Croat and Slovene distrust of the Serb elites. At various periods during the existence of a Yugoslav state the competition and distrust was between different elites (e.g. Serb and Croat) and was not shared by or communicated to the peasantry of the differing communities (Bennet 1995; cf. Ramet 1996), that is communities who differed along lines of language, religious persuasion and perceived descent.

In the post Second World War period the legitimacy of the Yugoslav state was based on the 'memories of the liberation war against Nazi occupation' rather than on communism, 'an ideology accepted by only a small minority of the population' (Sekulic 1997). However, throughout the 1980s and quite emphatically at the end of the 1980s, *the geo-strategic position altered quite dramatically*. Although the Serbs looked to the Soviet Union, as their Slav allies, Yugoslavia rested upon its independence from the Soviet Union, giving it a kind of freedom not experienced in Soviet client states. The decline and eventual collapse of the Soviet Union, and of the communist states tied to it, fundamentally altered Yugoslavia's geo-strategic position. The Soviet Union was no longer a threat but equally the West no longer 'needed' Yugoslavia as a buffer state between East and West. In this situation Serbia manoeuvred to transform Yugoslavism into Pan-Serbianism, a shift for which the Serb intelligentsia provided some of the justification in the mid-1980s (Pavkovic 1998; Magas 1993). Not only did they glorify Serb history but also portrayed Serbia and Serbs past and present as a victim state always in need of watchfulness against its multitudinous enemies and always ready to 'fight for its very survival'. The achievement of Serb aims within a federal Yugoslavia could only be by centralizing at the expense of multi-national autonomies; Yugoslavism was replaced by Serbian imperialism which, crucially, included defending 'imperilled' Serbs outside of Serbia, that is in Croatia, Bosnia, Kosovo but, equally crucially, scarcely at all in Slovenia.

Just as the West has lost interest in Yugoslavia as a buffer state, Western states (e.g. Italy) no longer pose a significant threat to Slovenia as the westernmost Yugoslav republic. As Sekulic argues, 'their [Croatia and Slovenia] main preoccupation became how to join Europe and not how to escape it' and now Europe had become 'attractive for the reform-minded, communist leaders of Slovenia and Croatia'. As

Europe no longer posed a threat (to Slovenia and Croatia) the real menace was now represented by Serb imperialism, thus reviving the long-standing conflict between centralism and the rights of the autonomous republics. The West seems to have been slow to recognize these new dispositions and was unwilling to recognize or guarantee a newly independent Slovenia (Janša 1994). It was reported in the *Guardian* that even in the 1990s a former British Foreign Secretary was involved in arranging finance for the Milosevic regime, enabling the sale and partial privatization of Yugoslav telecommunications, acting as a director of National Westminster bank (*Guardian*, 2 July 2001).

The account in the preceding paragraphs is largely, though not entirely, based on Sekulic's analysis. It is in sufficient detail to give a sense of his exposition of the idea of geo-strategy and geo-political position, and the Weberian notion of legitimacy; it also gives the core meaning of Sekulic's analysis. It is as well therefore to conclude this passage by citing directly from Sekulic's conclusions. Geo-strategy was important in both the creation and the collapse of Yugoslavia, but at beginning and end the geo-strategical position was quite different:

The geostrategical explanation is important in understanding the dynamics of the creation and dissolution of Yugoslavia. Geostrategy operates on three different levels. First on the level of international actors and their perception of the importance of the creation or the dissolution of an entity like Yugoslavia; Second on the level of the interaction of geostrategical considerations and internal elite strategies; Third on the production of legitimacy as the result of geostrategical success or failure. (Sekulic 1997, p. 177)

After the Second World War the Yugoslav state stood at a point of balance between East and West, retaining a kind of constrained good relations with both. Its legitimacy, Sekulic argues, did not rest on communist ideology. The regime, he suggests, 'was popular not because it was communist, but because it successfully resisted the Soviet communist pressure and created stability where nobody expected that it could be achieved'. This situation was transformed when the Soviet Union began to disintegrate:

> The disappearance of the Soviet threat removed the sources of internal legitimacy of the regime and allowed the explosion of pro-Western sentiments. Consequently the shifts in external pressures, the attractiveness of the West and the disappearance of the threat from the East, totally destroyed the internal consensus and Yugoslavia exploded under cross-pressures and the attractions provided by the changes in the geopolitical environment. (Sekulic 1997, p. 178)

As well as Sekulic's specific conclusions about Yugoslavia and his theoretical conclusions about nation-state legitimacy and geo-strategic position, it is possible to draw some of our own conclusions for the analysis of a situation (the dissolution of Yugoslavia) which has so often been cited as 'yet another' index of the revival of or importance of ethnicity or of the ferocity of ethnic tensions. It is, of course, nothing of the sort.

One of the first things to notice about Sekulic's (and Hoogvelt's and Wieviorka's) analysis is that he takes the category of the state seriously, more seriously than the category of nation with which so many cultural enthusiasts confuse it. The state as a social organism has real power which depends both on material command of resources and on legitimacy by way of popular support and a more or less elaborated ideology. The elaboration of state legitimacy is only partly promoted in terms of an (ethnic) conception of the 'nation'. In Yugoslavia the legitimacy rested on the memory of liberation from Nazism and on protection from Soviet pressure. Only the Serbian variant, which was to be the instrument of the dissolution of the federal Yugoslav state, was a highly elaborated statement of ethnic history, symbol, and mystical notion of destiny. And the Serbs had, after all, most to lose from the demise of Yugoslavia. The second thing to notice is that Sekulic looks outward rather than inward to establish an analysis of conflict in Yugoslavia. This is following Weber's recommendation that state legitimacy must be understood in terms of the state's relationship with external powers. But it is also a direct challenge to all those who have primarily looked inward, to the sociology and (ethnic) politics of the Yugoslavian state as the source of the explanation of internal (ethnic) conflict.

The third thing to notice is that following Sekulic's model it is possible to construct a highly theorized explanation of ethnic conflict *with very little reference to ethnicity itself.* This is for the most part an enormous strength for it shows that he, unlike a small army of journalists and ethnicity specialists, refuses to be mesmerized by the word 'ethnic' in the phrase 'ethnic conflict'. It is also a gap in the Sekulic account but not an irreparable one. What is omitted is any close-weave account of how the ethnicities 'Serb', 'Croat' or 'Slovene' are constructed both in the public imagination and in the routine exchanges of everyday life. In Sekulic's account the categories are rather taken for granted; what would complete the account would be (1) an anthropology of the construction of ethnic categories, and (2) an understanding of how, under the conditions Sekulic brilliantly describes, people came to choose to act and were forced to act in terms of these categories. People acted in this way under the conditions of Serb-led centralism which precipitated Yugoslavia's dissolution; they acted in accordance with ethnic boundaries despite the fact that these boundaries – in terms of language, inter-marriage and co-residence – had previously been indistinct, unimportant or both. Michael Banton's contention that 'ethnic conflict' may often be improperly so-called follows much of the same logic. This kind of analysis suggests why ethnic categories, being irrelevant or of low importance under some circumstances, become the principal points of reference in others (Banton 2000).

Post-Soviet Russia

Some of the same kinds of considerations are evident in an investigation of 'ethnic tensions and separatism in [post-Soviet] Russia' (Stepanov 2000). The author looks at a wide array of ethnic or nationalist conflicts in Russia and examines those *variable* conditions which might prompt ethnic conflict. Political, territorial and demographic factors are important: nationalist sentiments might be more easily mobilized when a region is a 'national' territory, and ethnic sentiments might be mobilized when distinctive groups live side by side in the same territory or when forced migration has disturbed a demographic and economic balance.

In the case of the North Caucasus we see evidence of the influence of what Stepanov calls 'contingent situations'. Two are especially important: the availability of arms and long-term economic crisis. The impoverishment of soldiers in the Red Army led them to sell their weapons, thus releasing arms into the population at large. The economic crisis placed increasing pressure on the countryside – where people might scrape an existence – and resulted in widespread overpopulation of the rural areas. The economic failure also produced populations of 'unemployed young men in the rural areas [which] further reinforces the incipient militarisation of the regions'. This becomes a powerful basis for an explanation of conflict without finally explaining why that conflict should follow the lines of ethnic boundaries. However, although Stepanov does not take these steps, the next steps are likely to be along the lines suggested by Simons (see above) and others. That is, under these kinds of circumstances, two things are facilitated or made more likely: (1) elite political leaders or organized military bandit leaders (or both in tacit collaboration) may gain advantage by drawing on ethnic symbols of collective identity; they may also gain from acting to exacerbate ethnic loyalties by inventing or perpetrating atrocities, and (2) individuals face situations where loyalty to kin or, by extension, 'ethnicity' becomes the 'sensible' choice, or virtually the only possible one in difficult or desperate circumstances.

Michael Banton has summarized this type of situation as follows:

[We may conclude that] firstly the significance of shared ethnic origin varies infinitely; secondly that it has to be considered in parallel with other potential bases for collective action including neighbourliness, and shared national origin, race, religion, and political interest. In local communities there are many such bases, making the relations between members multidimensional and enabling the different relationships to balance each other. When individuals are mobilised by appeal to shared ethnic origin this may appear to result in a distinctive kind of conflict but the underlying processes are common to many kinds of mobilisation. (Banton 2000, p. 496)

This makes it clear that it is 'mobilization' that we have to understand. What prompts people to mobilize, and what prompts them to mobilize around particular symbols of collective membership or communal sentiments? The discussion in this chapter of poverty and wealth on a global scale, of the power of states in general, and the ability – or will – of states to guarantee the security of its member people(s), showed how these economic and state-security factors form the material contexts for social action. It is the shifts, sometimes dramatic shifts, in the disposition of these material factors which lead people to act in accordance with previously submerged identities and loyalties. A pronounced emphasis on these *contexts of action* is necessary to avoid a mistaken emphasis on the apparently 'ethnic' nature of the conflict when the change in external circumstances results in communally oriented action.

This is important when the conflict is not only a matter of 'suspicion' or 'antipathy' but becomes murderous and ruthlessly violent. Then we need to understand 'why are people killing each other at all?' as well as understanding 'who is killing whom?' There are, in other words, questions of at least two kinds: why do people become desperate and violent, and who are the targets of violence and aggression? At least five conditions would have to be explored:

1 the way in which social and cultural differences are available as 'markers' between people;
2 the conditions under which these may be peaceful or non-relevant markers, as against critical moments when they are transformed into serious divisions;
3 the particular circumstance of a group's being seen as not legitimately present ('they have no right to be here'), as having things (rights, resources) 'to which they are not entitled', or as posing a threat to an 'inferiorizing' ideology;
4 the lack of restraint or the removal or collapse of restraint;
5 a reasonable expectation of impunity from violence.

The exploration of this set of conditions and potentialities would bring together the kinds of information and theorization of the evidence which permit a plausible theorization of what is often described as 'ethnic conflict'. The Barthian model (discussed in chapter 5) is principally directed at condition 1. The question of how ethnic identities originate, are articulated and sustained is only part of the story. We must also allow that although for some groups under some conditions, ethnic identities are brought into action, for many others such identities are scarcely formed, or are no more than loosely stated and frequently non-relevant markers. This requires us to consider when (if ever) ethnic identities are a source of action at all, let alone a totalizing and decisive point of reference for action and mobilization. Beyond this we are interested in when ethnic identities are not just part of a 'neutral' or benign pattern of difference, but are brought to bear as the main source of conflict and unequal power. Conditions 3 and 4 above, and the kinds of economic and political conditions we described earlier in this chapter, are the basis for the answer to these latter questions. This type of theorization is, of course, with the exception of condition 3, considerably less 'culturalist' than is currently the fashion in sociology. There can, however, be little doubt that the present emphasis on culture has been seriously overstated.

Summary

We drew on Hoogvelt's account of post-colonial (economic) conditions to sketch out some of the social environments in which ethnic identities may correspond with class niches. Economic changes may run counter to social policies for the amelioration of (ethnic) disadvantage. Thus in the USA equal opportunities policies may assist social mobility among African Americans and other minorities; de-industrialization and the disappearance of work decidedly runs counter to any such progress. In the latter part of the chapter we drew upon Simons' argument about Somalia to illustrate the idea of the precarious state; in precarious states ethnic relations are likely to be quite different from ethnic relations in stable states. We concluded by identifying principal steps in the development of a model of social change which can incorporate ethnic action and structure.

8

States, Nations and the Ethnic Majority: A Problem of Modernity

The previous chapter dealt principally with the economic and state-security conditions under which ethnic identities take on a heightened relevance. The conditions of utter desperation about material survival are most characteristic of parts of Third World countries where economic failure is a chronic condition. Allied to this, but not in any mechanical way, are the failures of the state machinery, that is the absence of any system of security guaranteed by the organs of the state, including but not confined to economic security. The first are a set of problems about *material survival*, the second a set of problems about *citizenship*. Both sets of conditions might prompt action defined by ethnic identity and often they will both be an influence together, even though one or the other will carry greater weight.

The problems of state security and material survival, which we addressed in the previous chapter, are most acute in (1) states with chronic economic dislocations, and (2) those states which have been subject to dramatic political shifts and failures of a regime. The first would include several sub-Saharan African states and some Asian states (e.g. Indonesia), whilst the second would include many of the (new) states of the former Soviet space and the Balkans. Some, like Indonesia, would certainly qualify on both counts. But, as Hoogvelt (2000) makes clear, the broad groupings of those who are (a) prosperous and who have defensible wealth, (b) employed, having a source of income but subject to exploitation and insecurity, and (c) economically and socially excluded – these broad groupings are also to be found in rich societies. In prosperous societies the position of the dispossessed is all the more alienating, being alongside people who are securely prosperous or super-rich. In the world's prosperous societies, the state *per se* is rarely 'precarious' but it still cannot guarantee the safety of its most disadvantaged members, including minority ethnic groups. People from these groups are typically liable to harsher and even arbitrary treatment by the penal system.

In the rich societies the conformation of ethnic, or racial or national identities is typically different from its counterpart in those societies where neither a stable economy nor state security can be guaranteed. In this chapter we will for the most part have rich 'First World' countries in mind as we look at some of the political, economic and cultural conditions of ethnic identity and its activation. In doing so we will take a particular look at the way in which the 'political-cultural' space is shaped in relation to *modernity*. This does not mean that, in contrast to Third World countries, problems of material survival and state security are absent and that therefore our analysis has to become political-cultural. But in states where material survival and state security are highly precarious, ethnic ties can be very compelling for those reasons.

Modernity and the nation

In chapter 1 we saw that the word 'nation', like 'ethnic group' and 'race', conveyed ideas about ancestral origins. These ideas of 'descent', 'origins', 'ancestry' and 'belonging to the same people' we found to be common to all three terms. The main meaning attaching to 'nation' particularly is the idea that nations and states are linked together. This may be in the idea that nations should be self-governing (i.e. have their own state). Or it may be in the idea that the people of a state necessarily are, or come to form, a nation. The latter idea incorporates the notion that the people of a state (its citizens) are not 'naturally' or without effort a nation, but they can become one by *building* a nation. The distinction has been made between *civic* and *ethnic* ideas of nation or nationalism (D. Brown 2000; Brubaker 1996). This is to distinguish an emphasis on the state and the legal rights and duties of people legitimately present within it, from an idea of a people with shared origins, a past and a future (even a destiny), for whom the state gives expression to their nationhood. These are opposite sides of the coin and in most cases civic and ethnic elements exist side by side; but it is an important distinction nonetheless (Fenton and May 2002).

The idea of nation

The idea of a 'nation' is at first sight a unifying idea. It expresses an idea of peoplehood which cuts across other divisions, especially of class and regional difference and inequalities. But both in history and in the present it almost always expresses some sectional purpose on behalf of part of the whole. In nation-formation there have been groups with a particular stake in the 'national idea' and in the present most nationalisms are in some way divisive. We look at the formation of nations (in Europe) in what follows, and initially we draw upon Liah Greenfeld's theory as a comprehensive account of the origins of the concept of nation (Greenfeld 1993).

Central to Greenfeld's account is the idea of envy and bitter competition between social classes – a set of social attitudes described as *ressentiment*. Out of this in England in the sixteenth and seventeenth centuries grew an idea of nation. There were in England, as the feudal order crumbled and a new class structure emerged, classes whose members felt insufficiently recognized, and classes whose members feared the threat posed by *arrivistes* (newcomers to power and eminence). There were upwardly mobile groupings within an elite, or seeking entry to an elite, who lacked respect and recognition, or the measure of political power which they craved. The mobile groups may be fragments of a new class such as representatives of newly rich men of trade and commerce, or fragments of an older class, the aristocracy. Among the aristocracy, newer entrants to the class go unrecognized by older aristocractic families. The 'new' aristocrats regret their lack of lineage and resent their less than full acceptance; the older aristocrats, especially if they are poor but dignified, bitterly reject the credentials of their new class partners.

This sociological model of class envy and status insecurity, to be found in sixteenth- and seventeenth-century England and eighteenth-century France, has two features of special interest to us. The first is that the (total or partial) exclusion of a new class creates the space for the idea of nation, since the upwardly mobile stand to benefit from replacing the conventions of aristocracy with an ideology of an 'open-membership' nation. The second is that the ideas of 'freedom' and 'equality' also serve the new classes, who benefit from the articulation of a 'national' society. The key to the emergence of a nation and of nationalism is the broadening acceptance of the idea of a single political community to which all belong. In England a string of related circumstances aided 'the spread of these ideas by growing numbers of people in different social strata'. The most important circumstances 'were the transformation of the social hierarchy and the unprecedented increase in social mobility throughout the sixteenth century; the character and the needs of the successive Tudor reigns; and the Protestant reformation' (Greenfeld 1993, p. 44; my emphasis). This period of unprecedented mobility was 'sustained for a hundred years or so'. Meanwhile the monarchy had an interest in 'the extinction of the old nobility' to be replaced by a new one which was more educated and drawn from many strata of society:

The redefinition of nobility . . . as a status based on merit, and not on birth, was a simple acknowledgement of this transfer of authority from one elite to another, which was virtually happening before one's eyes. A fundamental transformation of this kind required a rationalisation . . . It is at this juncture, I believe, that nationalism was born. (Greenfeld 1993, p. 47)

In France too resentments arose from competition between old and newer elements of the rich and powerful. The vulgar rich were maligned by the old rich but the aristocratic poor hated both: 'the most vehement detractors of capitalism came from among penniless intellectuals who did not make it into the elite ... and they hated the rich whose blood was blue as much as the rich whose blood was red' (Greenfeld 1993, p. 150). These status anxieties among the French aristocracy were augmented by feelings of envy towards England. Both sets of feelings contributed to French national self-consciousness. In the second half of the eighteenth century 'the aristocratic-intellectual elite in France was ... personally wounded by the superiority of England and felt *ressentiment* generated by the relative position of the country'.

In a later commentary Brown (2000) describes these and similar political sentiments as nationalisms 'articulated by an insecure class or status group' and being 'ressentiment-based' and usually illiberal. Greenfeld even suggests that these bitter feelings of loss or threat to status may be the clue to nationalism and thus to modernity:

[I]t would be no over-statement to say that the world in which we live was brought into being by vanity. (Greenfeld 1993, p. 488)

Greenfeld's comments are directed towards a group of nationalisms, associated with the formation of modern nation-states in Europe. There are many other nationalisms, including those of end-of-empire new and restored states; these followed the end of the British, French and Dutch empires, for example, in the mid-twentieth century and the collapse of the Soviet empire and the Yugoslav federation at the end of the twentieth century. But Greenfeld's analysis is important because it shows that nationalist sentiments are almost always linked, directly and indirectly, to a view of the future held by particular groups in a society; they are linked to social mobility and class position. Some groups have a special interest in the furthering of the nation and of a particular idea of the nation – however much 'all' may benefit.

Nation and majority

Understanding nations and nationalism becomes an essential step in understanding ethnicities in the contemporary world.

Racism and nationalism are not the same thing, the first focusing on an ideology of inherent difference (see Fenton 1999) and the other on the elevation of the idea of nation to the highest value. But they are frequently closely allied to each other (see Balibar and Wallerstein 1991) as we can see in ideas of empire, Britishness, and white England or Britain during and after the imperial period. Similarly an early peak of American imperialism, at the turn of the nineteenth and twentieth centuries, was marked by a surge of ideas about the manifest destiny of the (white) American people (Gossett 1965). These ideas are expressed *aggressively* when a nation-state proclaims its world mission – under the British empire, the white man's burden. They are expressed *mundanely* in the reiteration of what Billig has called 'banal nationalism', the daily acknowledgement of the flag or the repetition of the name of the country and the name of the people (Billig 1995).

It is seemingly inescapable that where a national self-image is strengthened it has a simultaneous effect of tacitly or actively excluding people defined as 'other'. This does not mean that the group self-consciousness of the minority groups is only prompted by the self-statements of the majority. Ethnic minority consciousness is not purely 'reactive', or reacting to hostility. But ethnic groups define themselves in a situation where others are defining them, often with some expressions of hostility, suspicion and rejection. Thus ideas of nation and ideas of who properly belongs to the nation are essential to the self-awareness of ethnic groups. There are no ethnic minorities without an ethnic majority. Anthony Smith (see discussion in chapter 1) is making this point when he writes: 'Even dominant ethnic groups must turn a latent, private sense of ethnicity into a public manifest one, if only to ensure the national loyalty of their members against the claims of other groups' (1981, p. 19).

In the contemporary world 'nationalisms' and 'racisms' are frequently found side by side and are often perfectly fused in a single ideology. This is the case with the nationalism-racism of the National Front led by Jean-Marie Le Pen in France (Marcus 1995) or the Serbian nationalism-racism led by Slobodan Milosevic in former Yugoslavia (Magas 1993). These racism-nationalism fusions usually contain four elements:

1 a sense of unwanted social change;
2 a latent ethnicity identifying itself as the nation;
3 a group, section or class experiencing a sense of threat, including a disenchantment with modernity;
4 the identification of one or more other identities as utterly different, unwanted or lowly regarded, and as the cause of social pathologies.

In these kinds of circumstances latent majorities and their racist-nationalist fusions are very important in both defining others and inspiring the self-consciousness of other groups. These latter groups then draw on their own resources to resist or redefine themselves in the public space.

The discontents of modernity: two accounts

Two accounts of racism, nationalism and modernity have stimulated and elaborated this kind of argument. One is Rattansi's essay ' "Western" Racisms, Ethnicities and Identities in a "Postmodern" Frame', and the other is Wieviorka's 'Racism in Europe: Unity and Diversity', both in *Racism, Modernity and Identity on the Western Front* (ed. Rattansi and Westwood, 1994). Students can also consult similar lines of reasoning in Balibar and Wallerstein (1991) and in Miles (1993). Wieviorka's work is also fully presented in his *Arena of Racism* (1995). Rattansi's analysis is intentionally 'postmodern' whilst Wieviorka's rests on an analysis of 'post-industrialism' and some profound shifts in modernity. This difference is of little importance; the common ground is an appreciation of certain accelerating changes in the modern world.

Central to Rattansi's analysis is the diagnosis of ambivalence in relation to modernity. In particular people seek 'freedom' and 'openness' whilst yearning for security and certainty; this is both a sociological and a psychological opposition:

modernity's ambivalence is generated not by occupying only the first term of the binary between 'order' and 'chaos' but by inhabiting both terms simultaneously – there is a striving for order while at the same time there is an excitement, exhilaration and anxiety produced by rapid change and the proliferation of choices inherent in modernity's discursive and institutional configurations. (Rattansi 1994, p. 25)

This ambivalence towards modernity is expressed towards ethnic targets where an ethnically defined group is regarded as the source of this ambivalence. An ethnic group is then identified as the cause of modern discontents. Thus in the central case of Jewishness and anti-Semitism the Jew is seen to represent all that is threatening about modernity – individualism, hidden capital, cosmopolitanism – whilst also representing the solidarity of the (Jewish) community, traditional family life and religion. Jews are then hated both as rootless cosmopolitans and as unremittingly loyal to their community. Unlike black Americans who are objects of racism and represented as 'failing', Jews are racist objects because they are too successful.

Rattansi takes up the case of the British Asian woman as another illustration of ambivalence: she is

at once the guardian and pillar of the 'tightly knit' Asian family – much admired, especially by the right, for its 'family values' and discipline – but also a symbol of Asian 'backwardness'. She is seen as subject to extraordinary subordination and, by her adherence to Asian conventions, is regarded as an obstacle to the assimilation of Asians into British culture [and] is also considered sexually alluring. (Rattansi 1994, p. 68)

Wieviorka and destructuration

In Michel Wieviorka we also find that racism is linked to private discontents and to our disposition towards modernity. In Wieviorka's case the central ideas are of a crisis in modernity and what he calls the 'era of destructuration'. Industrial societies, he says, 'are living their historical decline'. The prominent features of this decline are the closures of factories and workshops and, we might add, the rapid global reorganization of commodity production, communications and technical and professional services. For example, whilst numbers of workers engaged in commodity production increases sharply in many 'modernizing societies' at the expense of traditional modes of agricultural subsistence, in the rich countries of the established economies, numbers engaged in factory and mining employment fall sharply whilst a professional and commercial class grows to up to 40 per cent of the labour force. This provokes great re-orientations of class structures – and class *cultures* – in both established modern and modernizing societies. The consequences of this 'grande mutation' (Wieviorka 1994, p. 178) are both institutional and cultural or political.

The most important institutional change is the 'decay of the working-class movement as a social movement'. The political and cultural accompaniment of this is the decline of the universalist project of equality, justice and social progress. With the weakening of trade unions comes a reduction of workers' demands to purely 'selfish', self-protective ones, and weakened unions may often be unable to deliver even these. This creates a space which is likely to be filled, from time to time, by violence, populist ideologies, and spontaneous political actions and formations. Middle classes too are gripped by 'unrestrained individualism' (Wieviorka 1994, p. 181) or periodic bouts of populism; their insecurities prompt a fear of downward social mobility. And 'below' both the middle class and the employed workers are the socially and economically excluded for whom the routes back into paid employment are increasingly difficult.

This is matched by a marked weakening of the state's ability, or willingness, to soften the impact of a quickly changing capitalist industrialism. The gap left by the state's inaction is again a space likely to be filled by populism and racism: 'A second element of destructuration deals with the state and public institutions, which encounter increasing difficulties in trying to respect egalitarian principles, or in acting as welfare states' (Wieviorka 1994, p. 180). Most European states have conducted massive reviews of state provision which have made problematic the provision of pensions, health care and state education. 'Immigrants' or 'minorities' may be targeted by populist politicians drawing on the resultant insecurities; minorities are seen both as over-burdening the state and as being the undeserving recipients of benefits.

Political debate about 'welfare' and state benefits has throughout Europe and North America become ideologically linked to 'undeserving' beneficiaries of state spending, frequently framed in a racist discourse (Solomos 1993; Faist 1995).

National identity

The third element in Wieviorka's account is the emergence in new forms of the question of national identity. It re-appears 'loaded with xenophobia and racism' having lost its association with openness, progress, reason and democracy (Wieviorka 1994, p. 180). The same logic – of destructuration – prompts the expression of a series of communal identities which may be national, ethnic, religious or regional. They inter-stimulate each other, as the bold assertion of one excites the response of another. All three components of destructuration, the decline of social movements, the failures of the state, and the politicization of national identity as a communal sentiment, create a space for racism. This allows Wieviorka to speak of racism as constituting a set of relationships to modernity, sketched out in three scenarios (Wieviorka 1995, pp. 122ff). The first of these is *modernity triumphant* where racism is expressed as the doctrine or sentiments of the dominant countries or peoples, whilst non-modern peoples are seen in racist terms. The second is where *modernity is seen as threatening* and destabilizing; those who are hated are the bearers of modernity. The third is where *modernity is not rejected but is not fully embraced*, where people feel the competition of 'others' and fear loss of status – in one instance, the racism of the 'poor white'.

Britain, ressentiment and the sociology of nationalism-racism fusions

Britain is a post-empire society in which many people over the age of fifty were educated in a society suffused with imperial values. It is seen and sees itself as a nation-state which has lost power in the world and is accustomed to contemplating its own long-term economic decline. A new capitalist revolution was effected through the 1980s and 1990s which hastened the break-up of a relatively stable social order established by a post-war consensus on state welfare and some measure of state economic intervention. Conjoined with a radical market economics, an undermining of the welfare state and the decline of the public sector, there was an equally radical moral conservatism extolling the very family values which were undermined by the policies of unrestrained individualism in the economy (Levitas 1986). This propelled Britain away from a European model (such as that of Sweden and France) of restrained capitalism and public welfare, towards an American model of uninterrupted market freedoms and pronounced moral conservatism. This economic trajectory was followed quite radically in New Zealand, Australia, and somewhat later and less enthusiastically in other European states.

As discontents mounted in the 1990s and the Conservative government had all the appearance of exhaustion, what had previously been sufficient support to form a government was quite dramatically turned into a virtual rout in 1997. Their place was taken by a Labour Party which had shed virtually all claim to be socialist and now presented itself as the 'modernizing' party, setting itself to reform the constitution, devolve power to the component nations of the United Kingdom, and create opportunity for all in a land of opportunity which 'welcomed diversity'. In the mood of disgust with the Conservatives, who won no seats in Scotland and Wales, this modernizing doctrine was enough to effect a landslide for Labour.

Some elements of these social and political changes fit remarkably well with Rattansi and Wieviorka's diagnosis. We may set these out schematically:

1 *The destructuration of social movements*
   The period of high 'pro-capitalist' dominance in the political sphere in the 1980s had the intended effect of defeating the labour movement. It also propelled the Labour Party in the longer run to distance itself almost entirely

from a socialist project, so discredited did socialism appear by the end of the 1980s.
2   *The weakening of state welfare*
    Many kinds of social provision were either removed or placed under intense pressure and there was a long-running portrayal of people dependent on welfare (e.g. single parents) as morally deficient. The state also withdrew from major sectors of public provision, especially transport.
3   *Modernity, morality and racism*
    Modernity (capitalist modernity) was simultaneously *embraced* in the radical pursuit of economic individualism and global market freedoms, and *rejected* in its form as social diversity and individual moral freedoms. The appeal to working-class conservatism had been partly economic – through, for example, the hugely popular sale of council housing – and partly political, through the reiteration of nationalist postures about immigration and 'race', with the latter often coded as a crime issue (Solomos 1993).

We mentioned above the loss of empire and a sense of economic decline. The economic decline formed part of a generalized sense of a world lost. Some industries and companies were particularly identified with Britain or England; the sale abroad of Rolls-Royce, the virtual ending of a British car-producing industry, the near disappearance of a ship-building sector, were all understood as a matter of national pride as well as of economic change. The end of empire was also a matter of identity since it had been a primary association of 'Britishness' (Colley 1992; Davies 1999; Miller 1995). The conflict in Northern Ireland made yet another form of British affiliation problematic. We could add to all these things the growth in the number of so-called 'visible minorities', the membership of the European Union – which was destined to become the source of division *par excellence*, the decline of the monarchy, and the devolution of power to Scotland and Wales. All these things contributed to a public picture of a world changing out of all recognition; more 'privately' change was effected by altered urban and rural landscapes, the decline of high streets, the decline of traditional grammar and English usage, the fierce commercialization of sport, and an ever-growing fear of crime. This sense of change – unwanted change, not exhilarating progress – is a component of profound distaste for 'this modern world'. It is often expressed as dislike and even hatred for changes in the definition of 'who we are' and 'what we stand for'.

These elements all fed into an ever-increasing anxiety about national identity which, by the 1990s, was unceasingly on the public agenda. These fears were prompted by every imaginable facet of 'modernity', many of them driven by local and global capitalist logics. And the question of identity was also prompted by the specific question of 'ethnic diversity', put there by a polite version of the demands for minority inclusion. Ethnic minorities raised the question of national identity by challenging the tacit ethnic majority. A succession of specific events prompted the outpouring of British and English national sentiments. Three notable ones were the possible arrival of Hong Kong Chinese, the election of a Labour government (committed to devolution of power to Scotland and Wales), and the publication of a ('pro-diversity') report on *The Future of Multi-ethnic Britain* (Parekh 2000).

The media and politicians who are cited below serve to give a sense of this 'ambivalence to modernity' which is expressed both as racism and as anxiety about national identity. Although they are clearly on the right of British politics, there is little doubt that they speak for some diffuse and some identifiable constituencies in the British population (*Guardian*, 28 November 2000). These are not, in other words, 'merely' the extreme views of a handful of rightist figures. Some of them surfaced during the period of Conservative rule; others were phrased as attacks on the 'modernizing' zeal of New Labour.

In the first instance it was feared that the handing back of Hong Kong to China might prompt some Hong Kong citizens to come to Britain. This caused some consternation, expressed by many political leaders. A *Sunday Telegraph* article asked 'Will this be the death of England?': 'The Prime Minister visiting Hong Kong has encouraged hopes that the colony's 3.25 million British dependent territory passport holders will be allowed to settle here' (*Sunday Telegraph*, 13 August 1989). It went on to speak of the 'unprecedented

influx of Chinese' and the 'pernicious doctrine of multira-
cialism' which has 'so debilitated the English that they have
lost their voice and no longer think of themselves as the sole
possessors of England'. The English, they suggest, 'have
become the white section of the community'. All this has been
done (although nothing had been done and few of those who
subsequently left Hong Kong had ever intended to choose
Britain) 'without reference to the wishes of the English
people'. Multiculturalism has made immigrants 'colonists to
whom England belongs as much and as undeniably as it does
to the English . . . Britishness has come to mean nothing more
than the possession of a passport'. Switching effortlessly from
Britishness to Englishness the author speaks of an English
people rooted in the land: 'Bewildered by the transformation
of their country and saddened by a permanent feeling of loss,
the English people have taken refuge in the past. What sort
of England will our children know if Mr. Major accommo-
dates the Chinese millions?'

The recurring themes of this anxiety about national identity are ethnic composition, the familiar landscape and way
of life, British history, cosmopolitan attitudes, and, occasionally, 'Marxism'. The reference above to 'the white section
of the community' exactly illustrates the idea of a latent
majority becoming self-conscious. The Parekh report had
suggested that British identity needed to be reconsidered to
become more inclusive, that Britain as a multicultural society
needed to respect multiculture so that communities flourished
within an over-arching community. A *Daily Telegraph* letter
writer (14 October 2000) wrote, after the publication of the
report, complaining that he had not been consulted: 'My folk
have lived on this patch for 3,000 years. I would have liked
to be asked my opinion.' The previous day's leader had suggested that multiculturalism and socialism were in league:

Perhaps Mr. Hague's [the then Conservative leader] most valuable
insight is that this purpose is a new version of the Left-wing ideology that tried, without much success, to destroy British economic
freedom in the 1970s. . . . [The Runnymede Trust, the publishers of
the report] wants to regulate schools, businesses, police, the law, the
health service, newspapers and government so that 'diversity' – by
which is meant racial quotas and anti-British ideology – is enforced.

Britain, a further writer protested, 'is not some kind of hotel where people stay at their convenience' (*Daily Telegraph*, 11 October 2000). The people 'responsible' for these assaults on Englishness and Britishness were sometimes Marxists; they were also intellectuals, pro-Europeans, internationalists, and people who counterpose sophistication to 'what we really know' or to 'common sense'. Under the heading 'We know in our hearts what Britain means' Andrew Roberts wrote in the *Sunday Telegraph*:

The intellectual godfathers of the view that Britain requires re-branding are the historians Linda Colley and Norman Davies ... The rest of us simply know what Britishness is. When Professor Davies says that Britain is 'befuddled' about her national identity he might be speaking for metropolitan Europhile intellectuals, but most people are in no doubt about what Britain is and what it means to us. [referring to Colley 1992, Davies 1999] (*Sunday Telegraph*, 15 October 2000)

The *Daily Telegraph* also featured (13 December 1997) what it called the Battle of Britain in the classrooms, the fight for national identity in the school curriculum. The former government enforcer of standards in education, Chris Woodhead, wrote that the 'history we teach ought to be first and foremost the history of the British nation' and that 'English history must be central ... our education system ought to initiate all our children into the cultural inheritance which is England'. The failure to distinguish English and British is a notable feature here, as is the reference to *cosmopolitanism*: 'our young people will be given some watered-down cosmopolitan mish-mash – that would be good neither for people from other cultural backgrounds nor for ourselves' (*Daily Telegraph*, 13 December 1997). The phrase used above, 'for ourselves', is a good example of the latent ethnic majority.

A related and repeated theme is the idea that being British – or English – is now 'an offence'. The *Daily Mail* of 11 October 2000 (again just at the time of the Parekh report) wrote 'In praise of being British', and in 1996 the same paper had argued 'To be English in England today is almost a criminal offence' (*Daily Mail*, 23 April 1996). The Conservative

Party, in the run-up to the 2001 election, made a concerted effort to identify Labour with a 'cosmopolitan elite' living within 'the M25' (the M25 is a ring road around London: Hague actually once said 'within the beltway' which would mean nothing to most British listeners. The latter phrase derives from Washington, USA, and 'within the beltway' equally refers to cosmopolitan 'intellectuals' or 'liberals'). The *Sun* newspaper (24 October 2000) made a list of the 'metropolitan elite' who are 'trying to rule our lives' and 'don't like Britain and want to submerge it in Europe' (see *Guardian Editor*, 27 October 2000).

Significantly the *Financial Times*, the liberal mouthpiece of global capitalism, was one of the few newspapers to defend 'multiculturalism'. In 1997 they turned on a Conservative spokesman's attack on the multicultural society. In an article headed 'Bleeding hearts no, business heads yes' they warned that multiculture was popular with international capital, London being its heartland. One corporation after another is cited as liking London as a truly cosmopolitan city, where virtually every language in the world is spoken. 'We selected London because of the availability of foreign nationals' was the quotation from Delta Airlines (*Financial Times*, 12 October 1997).

The *Financial Times* was criticizing a former Conservative minister, Lord Tebbit, who has led many attacks on multiculturalism. His views, more than those of any other person in public life, illustrate perfectly a kind of ressentiment-based reaction to modernity where all apparent aspects of the 'modern world' are rolled up into a single framework: acceptance of homosexuality, liberal views in the Church, forgetting true British history, traditional moral values, crime and the city, multi-ethnicity, and Europeanism. Criticizing liberal elements of his own party, Tebbit wrote in the *Daily Mail* in the wake of the Conservative election defeat:

What is the Conservative party for? Why do I share a party with those who advocate sodomite marriage, membership of a federal state of Europe or the rejection of the hereditary principle? . . . New Labour is committed to multiculturalism. But unless we share standards, moral values and our national heritage we shall constitute neither a society nor a nation, but just a population living under the same jurisdiction ... Youngsters of all races should be taught that British history is their history or they will be forever foreigners holding British passports – and this kingdom will become a Yugoslavia. ... The British are not happy in our violent polyglot cities ... they have no wish to be ruled from abroad. (*Daily Mail*, 8 October 1997)

This statement virtually has it all – anger about liberal views on sexuality, anti-Europeanism, status anxiety (the hereditary principle), a nostalgic view of history and morality, a fear of multiracial Britain and a fear of crime ('our violent polyglot cities'), and ('no wish to be ruled from abroad') anxieties about power and 'international' threats to sovereignty. This sense of ressentiment in relation to modernity is connected to race, culture and nation. The anger is directed at a 'liberal elite' who espouse 'cosmopolitan values', a framing of political language which can also be found in the United States. In the period prior to the 2001 election, Hague, the Conservative leader who was much influenced by America, tried very hard to popularize the phrase 'liberal elite' in Britain, as a kind of diffuse cause of 'rising crime, the death of the family, single mothers . . .' (*Guardian*, 15 December 2000).

Most of this debate is within the framework of 'respectable' politics. Two brief instances will illustrate a continuity with a discourse beyond parliamentary circles and closer to the 'spontaneous' outbursts described by Wieviorka.

The fuel protest of 2000 was directed at high petrol prices in Britain and attacked the policy of high taxes on fuel. It was supported by farmers, road hauliers, independent lorry drivers and taxi drivers. For a short period in November 2000 it created a small crisis as roads were blocked (a tactic learned from French farmers) and fuel supplies were interrupted. The fuel movement quickly gained the support of the British National Party (BNP), an outright racist party, who stated that 'many of our members are hauliers, farmers and taxi drivers'. Not only did the BNP address the fuel issue, it also characterized high taxes as the result of 'political correctness', associated the Labour Party with homosexuality and described it as a 'government of perverts' (*Guardian*, 3 November 2000). A remarkably similar set of themes ran through campaigns associated with the defence of fox hunting at the time that the (Labour) government was planning to end it (*Guardian*, 30 September 1999). Posters and magazine articles attacked gay and black ministers or members of parliament, with posters reading 'Labour supports sodomy' and advising a black MP to 'direct her talents to advising her scrounging supporters on how to claim more handouts' instead of supporting the ban.

Racism, ethnicity and nation

There are two sets of lessons we can draw from these few illustrations. First, the sentiments expressed in many of these instances bear many of the marks of what we have described as *ressentiment*. These are ressentiment attitudes and they are ressentiment politics. Interestingly, there is no obvious pattern of class affiliation in the sociological source of these sentiments; they are not unmistakably 'working class' or 'upper class', but rather come from a series of fragments of classes or social locations. This is not to say that there is no class location: discontented farmers, taxi drivers, (anti-European and non-corporate) businessmen, traditional industrial workers made redundant or insecure, defeated right-wing politicians – all these provide hints of a series of social locations associated with ressentiment. They are periodically united in their loathing of a range of social changes which would include liberalization of the Church, women's rights, multiethnicity, reform of attitudes to sexuality, inner city crime, the banning of physical punishments, and the 'decline' of the family. In the absence of social movements, as Wieviorka argued, these fragments of classes embrace fragments of attitudes sufficiently to produce an illiberal whole.

The second lesson is that all the attitudes described here loosely cohere around ideas of nation, *our* people, our land and our way of life. Ethnic minorities are targets of dislike because they are not majority, and majority identity becomes important because it has become problematic. The other anti-modernism postures are then 'rolled up' together with racism in a unity, not just of racism itself as Wieviorka has argued, but in a unity of anti-modernity, where the hallmark of modernity is change and liberality.

Conclusions

In this chapter we concentrated on the way in which ethnic identities become part of national political discourse. In particular we wanted to show how the concept of ethnic minority group is dependent on the idea of ethnic majority. The idea of 'nation' and the idea of 'ethnic majority' are closely allied although the consciousness of the ethnic majority is often latent and tacit. An ethnic majority may mobilize because it sees itself threatened by the claims – for inclusion – of minorities. In this way racism and nationalism are frequently fused. Finally we suggested that in some sectors of the population, at key junctures in economic and political change, a resentful attitude towards 'modernity' is packed together with this fused racism-nationalism.

9
Ethnicity and Modernity: General Conclusions

As a general rule it should be understood that there cannot be a theory of ethnicity, nor can 'ethnicity' be regarded as a theory. Rather there can be a theory of modernity, of the modern social world, as the material and cultural context for the expression of ethnic identities. This is to reject all separation of 'ethnicity' or 'racism' or 'national identity' from the social and theoretical mainstream. It is to reposition the interest in ethnicity within the central domain of the sociological imagination – the structuring of the modern world, class formations and class cultures, and the tensions between private lives, cultures, and the cohesion of communal and public life.

A theory of ethnicity?

The argument that there cannot be a 'theory of ethnicity' has been sustained, explicitly or implicitly, throughout this book. The reasons for this are two. The first is that there is not a single unitary phenomenon 'ethnicity' but rather an array of private and public identities which coalesce around ideas of descent and culture. But the contexts in which these identities are found are multifold and multiform. This does not mean simply that there are 'ethnicities' rather than 'ethnicity', that it is the 'same' phenomenon in different situations.

Rather it means that the contexts are sufficiently different so as to give an entirely different sense, force and function to ethnic identities according to the social, economic and political site of their emergence or their rise to importance. These contexts have been identified as the migrant worker complex, the condition of indigenous peoples, post-slavery societies, post-colonial multi-ethnicities, and the contestation of national identity and dominance in established nation-states.

The second reason is that in the 'contexts of ethnicity', it is the context that matters more than the ethnicity. This we have illustrated by showing how the significance or salience of ethnic identities is, in many if not most instances, influenced by external co-ordinates of the ethnic action rather than by internal characteristics of the ethnic identity itself. This is not to write ethnicity out of the picture, but it is a serious demotion. It suggests that our attention should be primarily turned to these 'co-ordinates' which form part of an explanation of why 'ethnicity' has become a focus of action. This is true at the aggregate level where the question can be posed as 'how do we account for the fact that ethnicity has salience in the organization of private, communal and public affairs in the country, state or region?' It is also true at the individual level where the question can be posed as 'why does the individual act – in these or those circumstances – in response to ethnic prompts? Why in these circumstances is the individual's action oriented to ethnicity?' This is the classic posing of the sociological question by rational choice theorists (Banton 1987; Hechter 1995). Something, they are saying, must influence why an actor acts in accordance with ethnicity in this circumstance but not in that one. Our interest then is not just in 'ethnicity' but in ethnicity as a component of the sociology of modernity.

Ethnicity as theory

If this is why we are not seeking after a 'theory of ethnicity', the reasons why 'ethnicity' is not a theory are considerably more straightforward. The idea of ethnicity could only be theoretically dominant if any of three conditions were met:

1   if ethnicity is seen to be a source of motivation, or
2   if ethnicity is seen as the principal framework of social organization, or
3   if ethnicity is seen as a quite autonomous and fundamental principle of action.

The first is rarely the case although it is common to see problems of both human dignity or *recognition* and problems of social *allocation* significantly invested with ethnic meaning. It is true that Weber, in effect, tried to assimilate 'ethnically oriented action' to the category of 'affect': that is, it could be distinguished from rational action by the fact that ethnic ties were defined as 'emotional' rather than guided by reason or calculation. But much of the inclination of subsequent thinking about ethnicity has been *in precisely the opposite direction* – to assimilate 'ethnic action' to rational or instrumental action.

The closest approximation to the second condition can be found in societies such as the United States and South Africa where almost all social principles of difference are – or were – reduced to a single line of division along a binary black–white coding. Even in these cases where racial or ethnic difference is the dominant form of structuration it remains difficult to explain social change in terms exclusively referring to ethnic oppositions.

The third case is where ethnicity is seen as a primary source of action because ethnic difference is seen as being in some sense 'fundamental'. This is advocated by very few commentators although it is clear that in some social and historical settings, ethnic boundaries are very important indeed. Few people argue, in the manner of racial theory, that ethnic groups are basic population divisions. Van Den Berghe (1981) is an exception. He has argued that the inclination to act in accordance with ethnic group interests is a manifestation of a natural investment that the individual has in group preservation. This kind of social biologism has few supporters partly because the status of the concept of group is quite problematic. If we are to act in defence of a group that is 'ours' it must always be unmistakably clear which or what that group is. All the arguments, including the arguments in this book, about the situational and contextual

nature of ethnicity, would run counter to a biologistic view
of ethnicity.

Sociology of ethnicity: a phase of the sociology of modernity

The preceding section is suggesting that we should not be
searching for a unitary theory of ethnicity and, equally, that
'ethnicity' is not a primary or autonomous source of action
and structuration. The importance of ethnicity is conditional.
We shall, therefore, attempt to set out in this final chapter a
framework of argument addressing the problem of ethnicity
and racism in the modern world. This requires above all that
we essay a speculative sociology of modernity encompassing
the place of ethnicity within it.

In this exercise of theorizing ethnicity and modernity there
are, broadly speaking, two sets of arguments. The first set
deals with how ethnic identities are formed and how relationships with 'others' are articulated. The second set deals
with how these ethnic identities come to take on primary
importance *either* in particular circumstances, *or* in a 'totalizing' way. The key to answers to the first set of questions lies
in the historical accounts of slavery and post-slavery identities, of colonial and post-colonial social orders, of labour
and trader migration and settlement, of the conquest of
indigenous peoples in New World societies settled by Europeans, and of the articulation of the boundaries of sovereign
states with descent and culture communities. The work of
Barth and more recently Eriksen (Barth 1969; Eriksen 1993)
shows how people can and do relate to others in ways which
are designed to sustain the boundaries between communities,
and how people cope when boundaries are threatened with
a breach.

But the much wider questions are those addressed to the
problem of the 'activation' of ethnic identities, that is towards
understanding the conditions under which ethnicity becomes
important or even decisive in everyday discourse and
exchanges, or in the major political mobilizations in the
public sphere. This requires an outline of a theory of moder-

nity. It is, of course, only an 'outline', with selected features of the contemporary world singled out and highlighted, as they bear upon questions of ethnicity, nation and racism.

Late capitalism and modernity

In late capitalism the twin doctrines of economic freedom and political democracy are intensified both in depth and in breadth. The 'deepening' of economic freedom, in its implications for people as individuals, is in the perpetual raising of the material stakes for consumers: what was once desirable becomes indispensable. The broadening of economic and political freedoms lies in the historical progression of extending the scope of those to whom they are seen to apply. The inner logic of a doctrine that 'all men (and women) are created equal' is that exclusions are not justifiable; those who are excluded but nonetheless 'hear' the doctrine, such as African Americans or India's scheduled castes, are bound to find it an inexcusable and intolerable exclusion. The inner logic of a consumerist society is that no-one can be exempted from the material and psychological ambitions which are proffered.

Neither of these principles, one of *recognition* and the other of personal *accumulation* of material and psychological goods, can be realized. This is partly because they are in their nature unrealizable – we can never get enough recognition, we can never accumulate 'enough' – and partly because there are powerful contradictory tendencies in capitalist democracy. These two principles bear upon the politics of distribution and the politics of recognition (Taylor 1994). Ethnicity and racism in ethnic and nationalist politics are reinforced by the 'politics of recognition'. This would be true both of groups 'starved of recognition' and of groups (e.g. ethnic majorities) and classes who feel that their assumed pre-eminence is threatened. Ethnicity is tied into the 'politics of distribution' by the fact that access to resources follows ethnic lines.

The problem of material distribution is relatively straightforward. Late modern capitalist societies (capitalist, postindustrial economies with an ever-increasing power and range of communications media) promise more rewards to more people than can possibly be satisfied. At the same time there are dramatic shifts in the definition of who is useful and productive and of whose skills are needed. Hence whole classes or fragments of classes come to be seen as, and may see themselves as, 'dispensable' or outmoded. Even those who remain 'incorporated', either as the 'bankable' or as the employed but exploited classes described by Hoogvelt, may see their worth diminish or made precarious. This is a factor which we discussed in relation to ethnic groups in America: the deindustrialization of the USA has disproportionately affected groups who are least well situated to succeed in the postindustrial economy (for the relation between ethnicity, class and economy see Steinberg 1981, 2000; Wilson 1980; Fenton and Bradley 2002; Woo 2000).

Thus universalism (as for example a meritocratic and equal regard for all) cannot be sustained in a continuous, progressive and undiluted fashion. In Balibar and Wallerstein's (1991) phrase, switching back and forth from universalism to particularism forms the contradictory ziz-zag motion of capitalist modernity (in this context 'particular' means treating people by 'particular' criteria, including ethnic criteria). The wish to make best use of all talent and energy promises universalism; the wish to exploit some more than others leads to particularist super-exploitations of, for example, women and lowly regarded ethnic groups. Furthermore *some* of those who are exploited and subsequently made redundant (in Europe, typically, white males) belong to a 'privileged' gender and ethnicity but a decidedly disprivileged class. To some of them, the sight of temporary or enduring signs of success among minoritized ethnic groups and women is a classic source of ressentiment.

Furthermore the speed of economic change – for example the virtual disappearance of ship-building and coal mining from Britain within a generation, the rapid growth of super- and hyper-markets – is also accompanied by stark changes in the social landscape. These include in Britain's case the transformation of work, of neighbourhoods, and of the place of women. In work, craft skills and apprenticeships are lost, neighbourhoods become multi-ethnic, high streets lose their family butchers and hardware shops, and women appear where once only men were found. At the same time the endless search for material satisfactions, coupled with the inability of many to realize their aims, produces cycles of rising utilitarian crime (Field 1990). The bankable classes and especially the less-favoured but employed wage-earners are the bitter victims of these crimes. These changes in the social landscape are experienced as a 'loss of community', the loss of a world in which people did not lock their doors, nor fit alarms to their cars and houses, and knew their neighbours. These scenarios are 'racialized' or 'ethnicized' especially with respect to residential distributions, and perceptions of neighbourhood and crime (Solomos 1993).

The contradictions of late capitalist modernity

We have hinted at some besetting contradictions in capitalist modernity. The first is the contradiction between the idea of equality and the persistence of inequality, not only in outcomes (i.e. differential rewards) but also in opportunity, through the operation of class cultures and institutional closures. The second is the contradiction between individuation and 'liberation' and the idea of, and experience of, 'community'. A third is the contradiction between sanctity values (abolition of physical punishment, individual freedom of sexuality, for example) and control values, that is 'traditional' values relating to constraint and sexuality. Each of these contradictions has the potential to become deeply imbued with ethnic significance. We have discussed the imbrications of class and ethnicity, the ways in which groups are 'consigned' to particular economic niches. These niches also become, at least temporarily, ethnic niches. The clearest examples stem from economic migrations – of Filipina maids, Indonesian construction workers, and many other examples.

Wieviorka is one of the few writers to have addressed both the 'class problematic' and the 'community problematic'.

Wieviorka attaches primary importance to classes within capitalism; class-based movements are essentially 'modern' in form and in principle. But Wieviorka is also concerned with another and related dimension of the contemporary world, and that is the persistent tension between 'individualism' and 'community'. He is taking his cue from Louis Dumont's distinction between 'holism' and 'individualism' where Dumont (1986) first suggests that racism can be explained as a response to the transition from the former to the latter. Thus Dumont's account would be similar to other general accounts of the rise of a modern social order which view modernity as a 'loss of community'; this loss creates tensions which may be resolved by antagonistic or 'irrational' social movements. But Wieviorka is especially concerned not just with a transition to modernity but with *a persistent tension within modernity itself*. This concern, Wieviorka argues, is reflected in Dumont's later work:

The problem is in fact no longer seen as one of transition, or of the mutation of one societal type into another, but rather as involving the necessary and impossible cohabitation of two modes of thinking: the old holistic one with life still in it, the new individualistic one not yet triumphant. (Wieviorka 1995, p. 29)

This Wieviorka–Dumont framework provides us with a way of thinking about 'the individual' and 'community' within the setting of late capitalism. This necessarily enables us to think about ethnicity and nation, since these are identities and associations which are implicated in the way we think about the individual and the collective. Dumont's suggestion that racism can be partly understood as a consequence of a tension in modernity between 'individual' and 'community' could prove to be very fruitful. As Wieviorka suggests, the tension of holism–individualism becomes the basis of a theory of racism 'in terms of the dissociation it expresses between modernity and the particularism of the nation, or more broadly, the community' (Wieviorka 1995, p. 122). This argument could be generalized beyond racism to the general way in which national and ethnic identities are expressed and embraced.

Dissociation, exploitation–inequality: the politics of distribution and recognition

This way of thinking enables us to place an understanding of ethnicity, race and nation within a general understanding of modernity and changes within modernity; in other words, with a general theory of modern social orders. This requires viewing 'modernity' as posing problems along two distinct if related axes: one an axis of exploitation and inequality, the second an axis of isolation and dissociation. The two are recombined through the general principle of 'individualism' since this is, in the great traditions of sociological thought, a principle of an unequal economic order (a market economy) and a principle of social organization and culture (the breaking of traditional ties and the hallowing of the individual).

Individualism

Individualism was constituted *morally* and *culturally* by the cult of the individual. This was the growth of a culture in which regard for the individual and the sacredness and dignity of the individual became the ultimate human value. So the cult of the individual (Durkheim 1933; Fenton 1984), which could be equated to all those values which have been called 'universal' and the foundation of 'human rights', is a demonstration of a sociological 'law': the less that collective life embraces and enfolds the individual, the more the individual breaks from the 'natal milieu', the more society places a value on the individual. This value, or set of values, has the potential to be the foundation of a new civic morality and thus restore some of the moral binding power to a social order whose collectivities have been progressively weakened.

Two worlds – the liberal and the authoritarian

But individualism is also seen as the process of social detachment of individuals from communities, as fragmentation and isolation. Individualization is not simply a myth of modernity; *it has a foundation in the real experience of people*. At the same time it takes on many of the characteristics of a myth in the multiple portrayals of modern life as disruptive and destructured: in most contemporary Western societies, and many non-Western ones too, there is an abiding social imagery of a lost world of community, authority and trust. On this view, there was a time when 'people had regard for one another', 'children obeyed their parents' and no-one lived in constant fear of crime. This spectre of social breakdown is a repeated and powerful theme of both politicized commentary and everyday discourse; the fact that it is part of everyday discourse is the reason why political actors always suspect or hope that they can trade on these very fears, whether they share them or not.

But in the world of moral politics there is a further contradiction: on the one hand there is a broad group of values which comes close to Durkheim's civic morality rooted in regard for the individual, personal liberties, and freedom of conscience; on the other hand there is another diffuse set of values which places 'family values', authority, punishment and control at the head of its moral priorities and derives much of its momentum as a political force from its mocking rejection of the individualist principles. The first set are sanctity values, the second set are control values. *Sanctity* values endorse recognition of difference in, for example, sexual orientation; *control* values endorse punishment and mock the 'deviant'. Again this tension in the moral order of modernity is reproduced in ethnic and national settings. In ethnic minority groups, especially urban migrants, the country of new settlement is perceived as devoid of moral control. In the ethnic majority population, multi-ethnicity is combined with a view of 'loss of control'. These are arguments which we discussed in chapters 6 and 8.

Four principal problematics

Capitalist modernity, then, presents a series of interlinked problematics all of which are indicated directly or indirectly in the preceding passages. There is a *social class* problematic where the idea of 'equality', and in particular equality of worth and of opportunity, continually runs up against *de facto* inequalities of both outcome and opportunity. Sustaining ideas of equality under these circumstances is difficult. Those who gain least learn a contrary message from real experience. Furthermore the secure classes actively promote the idea that the 'failures' are unworthy and responsible for their own position.

There is too a *cohesion problematic*, described above as the contradiction between 'individual' and 'community'. There are real losses in community cohesion when the sociological processes of individuation press people more and more into 'individual lives' both materially and symbolically. The mobile telephone is one example of individuation, providing exhilarating individual freedoms, but also separating individuals from friends and family even when they are with them. Individuation is progressive, pushing the idea of individual freedoms to ever newer heights.

There is a *state and 'order' problematic*, which we discussed in chapter 6. In many newer (and post-colonial) states, the state is barely established as the guarantor of material and legal security, let alone of advanced individual rights. In 'established' states, the state machinery is the repository of procedures for the protection of individual rights; thus the state may make extraordinary interventions to defend a humane principle. Such was the case in Britain when the courts insisted on the release of juvenile murderers on reaching maturity. Here the state acted to protect individual dignity against a background of moral outrage. In other instances the state utterly fails the test of universality, as evidenced by the treatment of minorities in custody.

There is, fourth, a *morality problematic*, which transcends each of the first three. This lies in the opposition between sanctity values and control values. Sanctity values are the ones which are often seen as being 'on the side of modernity' – progress, individual freedoms, moral 'liberations'. Control values are the ones which are on the side of common sense, common experience and authority. Sanctity values vote for an end to physical punishments because they demean the individual; control values vote for punishment because it is 'common sense' that miscreants will respond to 'toughness'.

Progressive responses are grounded in the wish to realize universalism. Here can be found all movements of minority ethnic groups which are directed towards the realization of civil rights and the removal of barriers to inclusion and mobility. The fact that 'minorities' in pursuit of their interests also express the interests of everybody indicates that they are giving voice to values (universalist human rights) which are in principle held by all. Hence Martin Luther King was able to speak of realizing the American Dream; he was setting out the terms of existence for an America which was not just a better place for black Americans but a better place for all Americans. Most (but definitely not all) social movements, of under-recognized populations and of people who are socially and economically excluded, are capable of assuming this universalist voice. But responses driven by ressentiment typically press in quite the opposite direction. It is here that we find the links between ressentiment, modernity, racism and the crises of national identity. For some, the 'opening up' of cultural and political space to previously disregarded communities is precisely the kind of apprehension of threat which generates feelings of ressentiment. For the less advantaged or socially excluded the promise of recognition and mobility also poses problems of individuation and community. The solidarity of the community of those who are seeking recognition is threatened by success; indeed the successful individual may become the traitor who has forgotten his or her roots. This applies in the case of class, gender and ethnic identities.

Modernity and ethnicity

In the immediately preceding passages I have tried to sketch out some of the sociological themes of modernity – or late capitalist modernity – whilst 'trailing' themes of ethnicity through the argument. Although this is very much a 'contextualization' of ethnicity, nonetheless many familiar ethnic themes are apparent.

1 *Class and ethnicity.* Ethnic identities cannot be reduced to class experience but class experience and class culture give shape or form to ethnicity especially when class fortunes and ethnic fortunes are closely allied.

2 *Social mobility and individuation.* A key theme of much interest in ethnicity is social mobility and the effect of social mobility on ethnic solidarity. The same is true of residential mobility and community formation. By and large the sociological argument has been that social mobility undermines ethnic solidarity. The politics of equal opportunities are also about social mobility – rather than social distribution. The evidence of class–ethnic concentrations is taken as an indictment of the opportunity structure.

3 *Individual and collective dignity.* In disadvantaged ethnic groups the routine unequal treatment of group members means that individuals are likely to experience the slight on the group as a slight on themselves. The options are to identify and 'fight' or to disidentify in order to escape the prejudices towards the group.

4 *Gender and ethnicity.* In ethnic minorities the preservation of traditional values may mean the continuation of a pattern of gender subordination. This can mean that gender equalities are in tension with 'ethnic tradition'.

5 *Racism and ethnicity.* The social changes of modernity are met with both exhilaration and apprehension. The disgust for modernity among ethnic majorities incorporates change in the country's ethnic composition alongside change in sexuality mores, punishment laws and gender equalities. Rather dolefully this makes racism appear not as an aberration from modernity but as a feature of it. More optimistically, the ressentiment and control values do not always succeed; rather they remain in tension with sanctity values.

This merely sketches out how an integration of sociological themes of ethnicity with sociological themes of modernity might take shape. In the final paragraphs of this chapter we try to restate some principal themes of the book.

Ethnicity in its place

In this book we have attempted two things: first, to provide a clear introduction to the field of ethnicity; and second, to essay an interpretation of the place of ethnicity in the contemporary world. In the 'introductory' phase, mostly the first four chapters, we examined the defining meanings of ethnicity, ethnic group and closely related terms. We also outlined some central debates, including the question of 'primordialism'. We discussed the USA-based debates about the work of Glazer and Moynihan. In the 'interpretative' phase, mostly the later chapters, we addressed two key questions: *In what contexts are ethnic identities formed?* And *In what circumstances do these identities assume importance for structure and action?* This latter question contains within it the assumption that ethnic identities and cultural difference may be present in any society *but their relevance for action can change* quite dramatically for reasons which lie outside the ethnicities themselves. In this final section we will summarize and draw together the main arguments.

An etymological view of the terms 'ethnic (group)', 'race' and 'nation' showed that there is a very considerable core of shared meaning and that this refers to the idea of 'our people', 'our origins' and the concepts of descent and ancestry. Since ethnicity is always relational it can also mean '*those* people' with '*their* origins and ancestry'. The shared core of meaning is revealed by the fact that each of these words appears in the definitions of the other two. Ethnic group and racial group (or race) are particularly closely allied and there is considerable support for abandoning 'race' and replacing it with 'ethnic group'. The US Census, for example, has recognized these difficulties but continues to use the concept of race, whilst disavowing the idea of race as a biological classificatory system (Rodriguez 2000). Thus the US Census still uses a terminology (e.g. 'Asian', 'White or Caucasian') which is remarkably similar to the categories of nineteenth-century racial theory (Hollinger 1995).

It seems unlikely that this use of the term 'race' in the USA will be abandoned. First, censuses have an in-built conservatism because of the desire to have comparable data over successive decades. Second, federal programmes and resource allocation depend on data collection. In this sense 'races' are given real administrative and public reality in the USA. Third, the discourse of 'race' is so powerful and historic in the USA that groups have invested a lot of meaning in race terminology. This includes not just the idea of whiteness as a privileged ethnicity, but the idea of black or African American as a focal point of political struggle against disadvantage and oppression. Fourth, the material social relations – the distribution of wealth and power – of groups identified as black, white and other categories, remain embedded sociologically. It takes more than a change in terminology to alter that.

We discussed the most concerted attempt to sociologize the language of 'race', represented by the concept of 'racial formation' in the work of Omi and Winant. In this argument the central objection to the 'ethnicity' framework is not to the meaning of ethnic group but to two ideas which are linked to the idea of ethnic group in the USA. First is the notion of 'assimilation' and the suggestion that 'ethnicity' is part of an assimilation model. That is to say that ethnic groups are communities descended from (European) immigrants who follow a path of social mobility and absorption into an American mainstream. Second is the idea of 'equivalence' between non-white, especially African American, groups and European immigrants, which neglects the importance of racist ideology in the USA.

The first association, with an assimilation model, is not a *necessary* one, although Omi and Winant may be right to suggest that in the USA it is an *actual* association. But what is a real difficulty with both the first and the second association is the idea that ethnicity can only express 'difference'. Clearly the social formation of ethnic identities is not solely about difference; it is also about separation, segregation, the power of one group over another, social and economic inequality, and the significance of ethnicity for citizenship and the functions of the state. If the discourse of ethnicity is seen to emphasize only 'difference' it will overlook these more substantial social realities of political and economic power and inequality. A discourse of ethnicity must have a language and theorization capable of addressing the political and economic contexts of what we have called 'late capitalist modernity';

and it must recognize that difference often, perhaps *usually*, means unequal difference. If Omi and Winant are right, the US discourse of ethnicity is primarily about the social mobility of white European immigrants; this is not a discourse capable of dealing with post-slavery ethnicities. Nor does it address the importance to American ethnicity of the binary construction of whiteness and blackness.

This discussion led us to consider that in popular consciousness, in the political imagination, and in academic debates, the discourses and languages of ethnicity are influenced by the local setting. For example, the American distinction between 'race' and 'ethnicity' would have no obvious meaning in Malaysia where in English 'races' and 'ethnic groups' are used interchangeably, and in *Bahasa Malaysia*, Malaysia's official language, both are captured by the term *bangsa*. In the USA 'ethnic groups' has acquired an association with whiteness, and with the countries of origin of successive European immigrations; in the UK 'ethnic groups' has an association with non-whiteness. The idea of whites as an ethnic majority in the UK, which we discussed later, has scarcely taken hold.

In reviewing the debates about primordialism we suggested that these debates have conflated three analytically distinct issues. These could be summed up in three questions: are ethnic groups real, are ethnic groups corporate, are ethnic 'motives' calculated? The first is a debate about 'social construction' wherein ethnicities are not seen as somehow 'fundamental' but as dependent on the way they are defined by 'us', by 'them' and by the state. The second is about the extent to which groups and communities defined as ethnic have any form of corporate organization. And the third is about the nature of ethnicity as a calculated affiliation as against an unreflective status and identity. Here we drove a broad path right up the middle of these arguments. Ethnicities are, in our phrase, 'grounded' as well as constructed. Ethnic identities take shape around real shared material experience, shared social space, commonalities of socialization, and communities of language and culture. Simultaneously these identities have a public presence; they are socially defined in a series of presentations (public statements, assertions, images) by ethnic group members and non-members alike. These social

definitions are part of the continuous construction and recon-
struction of ethnic identities. The second and the third elements are in fact variable features of ethnic groups. They vary
from highly organized groups to what Nagata called 'diffuse
identities'. Similarly, ethnic groups vary in the degree of collective self-consciousness and thus in the extent to which individual and collective action is calculated or instrumental in
the pursuit of ethnic ends.

In the following chapter we looked at an instructive period
in the history of the idea of ethnicity: the work of Nathan
Glazer and Patrick Moynihan and particularly the debates
surrounding their *Beyond the Melting Pot*, a study of ethnic
groups in New York City. In a retrospective consideration of
this work two problems stood out. The first was the failure
to recognize the special position of African American ethnicity, in the light of the centrality of the binary white–black
division in the USA. The second was the unexpected (by
Glazer and Moynihan) continuation of large-scale immigration into New York, especially from Puerto Rico, Central and
South America and the Caribbean. These new migrations and
the increased importance of immigration from countries of
Asia to the USA have radically altered the perspectives on ethnicity. In the latter part of the chapter we examined the work
of the anthropologist Fredrik Barth, writing at much the same
time (the late 1960s), whose work has made an enduring contribution via the concept of ethnic boundary. This suggests
that the crucial social action is the maintenance of boundaries in the relationship of ethnic groups. This represents a
significant shift away from a conceptualization of ethnic
groups as groups who differ by culture.

The later chapters of the book (6–9) shift the attention
away from an account of key terms of the subject and key
items of the literature, and towards explanatory and interpretative models. The emphasis here is on the exploration
of the sociological conditions of ethnically informed action
and structure. One of these conditions is the movements of
peoples within countries, from country to country, and across
regions and continents. These movements have been both
under compulsion and voluntary and all the historical evidence suggests that this difference is crucial to subsequent
social outcomes (Ogbu 1987; Steinberg 2000). Some of these

movements were established during the period of New World slavery (Degler 1971; Marx 1998), some during the colonial regimes of the nineteenth century and the first half of the twentieth century (Fenton 1999), and yet others in the great nineteenth-century migrations from Europe to North America (Handlin 1973). Most of these migrations were of agricultural and industrial workers. Some were movements of traders, such as the establishment of Chinese trading communities in South East Asia. By the end of the twentieth and the start of the new century, these labouring and trader migrants are being joined by professional workers who migrate to the nodal points of demand for intellectual and professional services (Castles 2000).

People who move in this way clearly 'carry with them' cultural and visible differences which become established as group differences in the new context. These movements also have a class character so that migrant groups acquire a class *and* ethnic distinctiveness (e.g. Jamaican nurses in Britain). A great deal of the sociology of ethnic groups is concerned with the class position and social mobility of migrants. As John Rex has correctly argued (Rex and Tomlinson 1979) indigenous workers are likely to protect their own class gains against the claims of newcomers. This question takes on significance in social policy too, as governments give formal backing to 'equal opportunities' for minorities. Thus 'ethnic relations' take on a class character, and class processes take on an ethnic character.

In chapter 7 the main 'conditions' of ethnicity which we examined were the insecurity of the state and global inequalities. In insecure or precarious states individuals cannot rely upon the rule of law to protect them physically, materially or in terms of civic human rights. Where ethnic, regional, cultural and language differences exist, these provide an alternative support and system of trust. Under these circumstances, and especially if the state itself is closely identified with one ethnic (regional, language) group, ethnic group affiliation can become not just important but crucial.

In chapter 8 we traced out a sociology of late capitalist modernity in which majority and minority ethnicities are politicized within the contexts of modern discontents. This, we argued (chapter 9), was an illustration of the need to integrate the sociology of ethnicity with the sociology of modernity. In this argument the fusion of ethnicity with nationalism and racism is made evident.

We have therefore, in this book, sought to clarify the meaning of the discourse of ethnicity, and its closely related discourses of race and racism and nationalism. We have done so by seeking to embed the sociology of ethnicity in a broader sociological discourse.

Bibliography

Afshar H. and Maynard M., 2000, Special Issue, Gender and Ethnicity, *Ethnic and Racial Studies*, 23(5), September.

Alba R., 2000, *Beyond the Melting Pot* 35 years later: on the relevance of a sociological classic for the immigration Metropolis of today, *International Migration Review*, 34(1): 243–79.

Alba R. and Nee V., 1997, Rethinking assimilation theory for a new era of immigration, *International Migration Review*, 31(4): 826–74.

Anderson B., 1983, *Imagined Communities: Reflections on the Origin and Spread of Nationalism*, London: Verso.

Anderson E., 2000, *Beyond the Melting Pot* reconsidered, *International Migration Review*, 34(1): 262–70.

Anthias F. and Yuval-Davis N. in association with Cain H., 1992, *Racialised Boundaries: Race, Nation, Gender, Colour and Class and the Anti-racist Struggle*, London: Routledge.

Balibar E. and Wallerstein I., 1991, *Race, Nation, Class: Ambiguous Identities*, London: Verso.

Ballard R., 1994, *Desh Pardesh: The South Asian Presence in Britain*, London: Hurst.

Ballard R. and Ballard C., 1977, The Sikhs: the development of South Asian settlements in Britain, in Watson J. L. (ed.), *Between Two Cultures: Migrants and Minorities in Britain*, Oxford: Blackwell, pp. 21–56.

Banks M., 1996, *Ethnicity: Anthropological Constructions*, London: Routledge.

Banton M., 1977, *The Idea of Race*, London: Tavistock.

Banton M., 1987, *Racial Theories*, Cambridge: Cambridge University Press.

Banton M., 2000, Ethnic conflict, *Sociology*, 34: 481–98.

Barot R., Bradley H. and Fenton S. (eds), 1999, *Ethnicity, Gender and Social Change*, London: Palgrave.

Barret J. and Roediger D., 1997, Inbetween people: race, nationality and the 'New Immigrant' working class, *Journal of American Ethnic History*, Spring: 3–43.

Barth F. (ed.), 1969, *Ethnic Groups and Boundaries: The Social Organisation of Culture Difference*, London: Allen and Unwin.

Barzun J., 1965, *Race: A Study in Superstition*, New York: Harper and Row.

Baudrillard J., 1998, *The Consumer Society: Myths and Structures*, London: Sage.

Bennett C., 1995, *Yugoslavia's Bloody Collapse: Causes, Course and Consequences*, London: Hurst.

Billig M., 1995, *Banal Nationalism*, London: Sage.

Boas F., 1982, *Race, Language and Culture*, Chicago: University of Chicago Press.

Bourdieu P., 1990, *In Other Words: Essays towards a Reflexive Sociology*, Cambridge: Polity.

Bradley H., 1996, *Fractured Identities: Changing Patterns of Inequality*, Cambridge: Polity.

Brass P. R. (ed.), 1985, *Ethnic Groups and the State*, Beckenham: Croom Helm.

Brass P. R., 1991, *Ethnicity and Nationalism: Theory and Comparison*, New Delhi: Sage.

Brown C., 1984, *Black and White Britain: The Third PSI Survey*, London: Heinemann.

Brown C. and Gay P., 1985, *Racial Discrimination: 17 Years after the Act*, London: Policy Studies Institute.

Brown D., 2000, *Contemporary Nationalism: Civic, Ethnic and Multicultural Politics*, London: Routledge.

Brubaker R., 1996, *Nationalism Reframed: Nationhood and the National Question in the New Europe*, Cambridge: Cambridge University Press.

Bulmer M. and Solomos J. (eds), 2000, *Racism*, Oxford: Oxford University Press.

Camejo P., 1976, *Racism Revolution Reaction, 1861–1877*, New York: Monda Press.

Carmichael S. with Hamilton C., 1976, *Black Power: The Politics of Liberation in America*, New York: Vintage Books.

Carter B., Harris C. and Joshi S., 1987, The 1951–55 Conservative government and the racialisation of black immigration, *Immigrants & Minorities*, 6(3): 335–47.

200 *Bibliography*

Cashmore E. E., 1987, *The Logic of Racism*, London: Allen and Unwin.

Castles S., 2000, *Ethnicity and Globalisation*, London: Sage.

Castles S. and Miller M. J., 1993, *The Age of Migration: International Population Movements in the Modern World*, Basingstoke: Macmillan.

Ceil J. W., 1982, *The Highest Stage of White Supremacy: The Origins of Segregation in South Africa and the American South*, Cambridge: Cambridge University Press.

Cohen A. (ed.), 1974, *Urban Ethnicity*, London: Tavistock.

Colley L., 1992, *Britons: Forging the Nation 1707–1837*, New Haven, CT and London: Yale University Press.

Conversi D., 2000, Autonomous communities and the ethnic settlement in Spain, in Ghai Y. (ed.), *Autonomy and Ethnicity: Negotiating Competing Claims in Multi-ethnic States*, Cambridge: Cambridge University Press, pp. 122–46.

Coope A. E. (ed.), 1993, *Hippocrene Standard Dictionary: Malay–English, English–Malay Dictionary*, New York: Hippocrene Books.

Cornell S., 1996, The variable ties that bind: content and circumstance in ethnic processes, *Ethnic and Racial Studies*, 19(2): 265–89.

Dahya B., 1974, The nature of Pakistani ethnicity in industrial cities in Britain, in Cohen A. (ed.), *Urban Ethnicity*, London: Tavistock.

Daily Mail, 23 April 1996, To be English in England is almost a criminal offence (Richard Littlejohn).

Daily Mail, 8 October 1997, What is the Conservative Party for? (Lord Tebbit).

Daily Mail, 11 October 2000, In praise of being British (Paul Johnson).

Daily Telegraph, 13 December 1997, New Battle of Britain fought in classrooms (Graham Turner).

Daily Telegraph, 11 October 2000, Britain is not some kind of hotel (letter to the Editor).

Daily Telegraph, 13 October 2000, Turning point at Runnymede (Editorial).

Daily Telegraph, 14 October 2000, The British question (letter to the Editor).

Davies N., 1999, *The Isles, a History*, London: Macmillan.

Davis A., Gardner B. and Gardner M., 1941, *Deep South: A Social Anthropological Study of Caste and Class*, Chicago: University of Chicago Press.

Degler C. N., 1971, *Neither Black Nor White: Slavery and Race Relations in Brazil and the United States*, New York: Macmillan.

Dollard J., 1937, *Caste and Class in a Southern Town: White Caste Aggression against Negroes*, New York: Doubleday.

Dumont L., 1986, *Essays on Individualism: Modern Ideology in Anthropological Perspective*, Chicago: University of Chicago Press.

Durkheim E., 1893, *De la division du travail social*, Paris: Alcan.

Durkheim E., 1933, *The Division of Labour in Society*, New York: Macmillan.

Eller J. D. and Coughlan R. M., 1993, The poverty of primordialism: the demystification of ethnic attachments, *Ethnic and Racial Studies*, 16(2): 185–202.

Epstein A. L., 1978, *Ethos and Identity*, London: Tavistock.

Eriksen T. H., 1993, *Ethnicity and Nationalism: Anthropological Perspectives*, London: Pluto Press.

Evans-Pritchard E. E., 1962, *Essays in Social Anthropology*, London: Faber.

Faist T., 1995, Ethnicization and racialization of welfare-state politics in Germany and the USA, *Ethnic and Racial Studies*, 18(2), April.

Fenton S., 1980, Race, class and politics in the work of Émile Durkheim, in *Sociological Theories, Race and Colonialism*, Paris: UNESCO, pp. 43–82.

Fenton S., 1981, Robert Park: his life and sociological imagination, *New Community*, 60(2), Autumn.

Fenton S., 1984, *Durkheim and Modern Sociology*, Cambridge: Cambridge University Press.

Fenton S., 1996, Counting ethnicity: social groups and official categories, in Levitas R. and Guy W. (eds), *Interpreting Official Statistics*, London: Routledge, pp. 143–65.

Fenton S., 1999, *Ethnicity: Racism, Class and Culture*, London: Macmillan.

Fenton S. and Bradley H. (eds), 2002, *Ethnicity and Economy: 'Race and Class' Revisited*, London: Palgrave.

Fenton S., Carter J. and Modood T., 2000, Ethnicity and academia: closure models, racism models and market models, *Sociological Research Online*, 5(2), <http://www.socresonline.org.uk/5/2/fenton.html>.

Fenton S. and May S. (eds), 2002, *Ethnonational Identities*, London: Palgrave.

Field S., 1990, *Trends in Crime and Their Interpretation*, London: HMSO.

Financial Times, 12 October 1997, Bleeding hearts no, business heads yes (Clay Harries).

Fleras A. and Elliot J. L., 1992, *The Nations Within: Aboriginal State Relations in Canada, the United States, and New Zealand*, Toronto: Oxford University Press.

Fleras A. and Spoonley P., 2000, *Recalling Aotearoa: Indigenous Politics and Ethnic Relations in New Zealand*, Oxford: Oxford University Press.

Foner N., 2000, *Beyond the Melting Pot* three decades later: recent immigrants and New York's ethnic mixture, *International Migration Review*, 34(1).

Fredrickson G. M., 1972, *The Black Image in the White Mind: The Debate on Afro American Character and Destiny, 1817–1914*, New York: Torchbook, Harper and Row.

Fredrickson G. M., 1988, *The Arrogance of Race: Historical Perspectives on Slavery, Racism and Social Inequality*, Hanover, NH: Wesleyan University Press.

Gans H., 1979, Symbolic ethnicity: the future of ethnic groups and culture in America, *Ethnic and Racial Studies*, 2(1): 1–20.

Gans H., 1994, Symbolic ethnicity and symbolic religiosity: towards a comparison of ethnic and religious acculturation, *Ethnic and Racial Studies*, 17(4): 577–92.

Geertz C., 1973, *The Interpretation of Cultures*, New York: Basic Books.

Ghai Y., 2000, *Autonomy and Ethnicity: Negotiating Competing Claims in Multi-ethnic States*, Cambridge: Cambridge University Press.

Gil-White F. J., 1999, How thick is blood? The plot thickens . . . if ethnic actors are primordialists, what remains of the circumstantialist/primordialist controversy? *Ethnic and Racial Studies*, 22(5): 789–820.

Glazer N., 2000, On *Beyond the Melting Pot*, 35 years after, *International Migration Review*, 34(1): 270–9.

Glazer N. and Moynihan D. P., 1963, *Beyond the Melting Pot*, Cambridge, MA: Harvard University Press (reprinted 1970, MIT Press).

Glazer N. and Moynihan D. P. (eds), 1975, *Ethnicity: Theory and Experience*, Cambridge, MA: Harvard University Press.

Goddard V. A., Llobera J. R. and Shore C. (eds), 1994, *The Anthropology of Europe: Identities and Boundaries in Conflict*, Oxford: Berg.

Gordon M., 1964, *Assimilation in American Life: The Role of Race, Religion, and National Origins*, New York: Oxford University Press.

Gossett T. F., 1965, *Race, the History of an Idea in America*, New York: Schocken Books.

Greenfeld L., 1993, *Nationalism: Five Roads to Modernity*, Cambridge, MA: Harvard University Press.

Guardian, *The Guardian Editor*, 27 October 2000, What *The Sun* said about the metropolitan elite.

Guardian, 30 September 1999, War over hunting turns dirty with smears against gay and black MPs (David Hencke and Kevin Maguire).

Guardian, 3 November 2000, Fuel protest website 'backed by BNP' (Simon Jeffery).

Guardian, 28 November 2000, The rise of the Little Englanders (John Carvel).

Guardian, 15 December 2000, Looking for an enemy (Polly Toynbee).

Guardian, 2 July 2001, Serbs question Hurd's role in helping regime (Ian Traynor).

Guardian, 14 August 2001, Lifting the veil (Angelique Chrisafis).

Guardian, 16 August 2002, Mahatir's migrant labours (John Aglionby).

Guiberneau M., 1999, *Nations without States: Political Communities in a Global Age*, Cambridge: Polity.

Guiberneau M. and Rex J., 1997, *The Ethnicity Reader: Nationalism, Multiculturalism and Migration*, Cambridge: Polity.

Guy W. (ed.), 2001, *Between Past and Future: The Roma of Central and Eastern Europe*, Hatfield: University of Hertfordshire Press.

Hall J. A., 1998, *The State of the Nation: Ernest Gellner and the Theory of Nationalism*, Cambridge: Cambridge University Press.

Handlin O., 1973, *The Uprooted*, Boston: Little, Brown.

Hechter M., 1995, Explaining nationalist violence, *Nations and Nationalism*, Part 1, March.

Held D. and McGrew A. (eds), 2000, *The Global Transformations Reader*, Cambridge: Polity.

Hirschman C., 1986, The meaning and measurement of ethnicity in Malaysia, *Journal of Asian Studies*, 46(3): 552–82.

Hirschman C., 1987, The making of race in colonial Malaya: political economy and racial ideology, *Sociological Forum*, 1(2): 330–61.

Hirschman C., Alba R. and Farley R., 2000, The meaning and measurement of race in the US Census: glimpses into the future, *Demography*, 37(3): 381–93.

Hirst P. and Thompson G., 1999, *Globalisation in Question*, Cambridge: Polity.

Hobsbawm E. and Ranger T. (eds), 1983, *The Invention of Tradition*, Cambridge: Cambridge University Press.

Hollinger D. A., 1995, *Postethnic America: Beyond Multiculturalism*, New York: Basic Books.

Hoogvelt A., 2000, Globalisation and the postcolonial world, in Held D. and McGrew A. (eds), *The Global Transformations Reader*, Cambridge: Polity, pp. 355–60.

Horowitz D. L., 1989, Incentives and behavior in the ethnic politics of Sri Lanka and Malaysia, *Third World Quarterly*, 14(4): 18–35.

Hughey M. W., 1998, *New Tribalisms: The Resurgence of Race and Ethnicity*, London: Macmillan.

Husbands C. T., 1991, The support for the Front National: analyses and findings, *Ethnic and Racial Studies*, 14(3), July.

Hutchinson J. and Smith A. D. (eds), 1996, *Ethnicity*, Oxford: Oxford University Press.

Huxley J. and Haddon A. C., 1935, *We Europeans*, London: Cape.

Jacobson J., 1997a, Perceptions of Britishness, *Nations and Nationalism*, 3(2): 181–200.

Jacobson J., 1997b, Religion and ethnicity: dual and alternative sources of identity among young British Pakistanis, *Ethnic and Racial Studies*, 20(2): 238–56.

Jacobson M. F., 2001, *Whiteness of a Different Color*, Cambridge, MA: Harvard University Press. (First published 1998.)

Janša J., 1994, *The Making of the Slovenian State, 1988–1992: The Collapse of Yugoslavia*, Ljubljana: Mladinska Knijga Publishing House.

Jenkins R., 1997, *Rethinking Ethnicity: Arguments and Explorations*, London: Sage.

Jordan W., 1968, *White Over Black*, Baltimore, MD: Penguin.

Kasinitz P., 2000, *Beyond the Melting Pot*: the contemporary relevance of a classic? *International Migration Review*, 34(1): 248–55.

Lawson S., 1992, Constitutional change in Fiji, the apparatus of justification, *Ethnic and Racial Studies*, 15(1): 61–84.

Lawson S., 1997, *The Failure of Democratic Politics in Fiji*, Oxford: Oxford University Press.

Layton-Henry Z., 1984, *The Politics of Race in Contemporary Britain*, London: Allen and Unwin.

Leach E. R., 1982, *Social Anthropology*, Glasgow: Fontana.

Lee D. J. and Turner B. S., 1996, *Conflicts about Class: Debating Inequality in Late Industrialism*, Harlow: Longman.

Lee S. M., 1993, Racial classification in the US Census 1890–1990, *Ethnic and Racial Studies*, 16(1): 75–94.

Leigh M., 1974, *The Rising Moon: Political Change in Sarawak*, Sydney: Sydney University Press.

Leigh M., 1975, *The Population of Sarawak: Baseline Rural Mapping of Rural Ethnic Distribution prior to the New Economic Policy*, Sarawak Gazette 1975–1976; reprinted in Monographs of Institute of East Asian Studies, University of Malaysia, Sarawak, 2000.

Levitas R. (ed.), 1986, *The Ideology of the New Right*, Cambridge: Polity.

Liddell, H. G. and Scott, R., 1897, *A Greek–English Lexicon*, Oxford: Clarendon Press.

Lott J., 1998, *Asian Americans: From Racial Category to Multiple Identities*, London: Altamira Press.

Lyman S. M., 1998, The race question and liberalism: casuistries in American constitutional law, in Hughey M. W. (ed.), *New Tribalisms: The Resurgence of Race and Ethnicity*, London: Macmillan, pp. 97–172.

MacDonald S. (ed.), 1993, *Inside European Identities*, Oxford: Berg.

Magas B., 1993, *The Destruction of Yugoslavia: Tracing the Break Up 1980–1992*, London: New Left Books.

Malik K., 1996, *The Meaning of Race: Race, History and Culture in Western Society*, London: Macmillan.

Marcus J., 1995, *The National Front and French Politics: The Resistible Rise of Jean-Marie Le Pen*, New York: New York University Press.

Marx A. W., 1998, *Making Race and Nation: A Comparison of South Africa, the United States and Brazil*, Cambridge: Cambridge University Press.

McCrone D., 1998, *The Sociology of Nationalism: Tomorrow's Ancestors*, New York: Routledge.

Miles R., 1989, *Racism*, London: Routledge.

Miles R., 1993, *Racism after 'Race Relations'*, London: Routledge.

Miller D., 1995, Reflections on British national identity, *New Community*, 21(2): 153–66.

Milne R. S. and Mauzy D. K., 1999, *Malaysian Politics under Mahatir*, London and New York: Routledge.

Mirza H. S. (ed.), 1997, *Black British Feminism, a Reader*, London: Routledge.

Modood T., 1992, *'Not easy being British': Colour, Culture and Citizenship*, London: Trentham Books and Runnymede Trust.

Modood T., Berthoud R., Lakey J., Nazroo J., Smith P. et al., 1997, *Ethnic Minorities in Britain, Diversity and Disadvantage*, London: Policy Studies Institute.

Morris H. S., 1968, Ethnic groups, in Sills D. L. (ed.), *International Encyclopaedia of the Social Sciences*, New York: Macmillan/Free Press.

Nagata J. A., 1974, What is a Malay? Situational selection of ethnic identity in a plural society, *American Ethnologist*, 1(2): 331–50.

Nagata J. A., 1981, In defence of ethnic boundaries: the changing myths and charters of Malay identity, in Keyes C. (ed.), *Ethnic Change*, Seattle: University of Washington Press, pp. 87–116.

New Straits Times, 1 December 2000, BN committed to ethnic co-operation despite loss.

New Straits Times, 17 April 2001, Bumiputera traders must be bold and emulate other races to succeed.

New Straits Times, 19 April 2001, Chinese seek knowledge earnestly, Malays don't.

Nisbet R. A., 1967, *The Sociological Tradition*, London: Heinemann Educational.

Ogbu J., 1987, Variability in minority school performance: a problem in search of an explanation, *Anthropology and Education Quarterly*, 18: 312–14.

Omi M. and Winant H., 1986, *Racial Formation in the United States*, London: Routledge and Kegan Paul.

Oxford English Dictionary: Compact Edition, 1993, London: BCA/Oxford University Press.

Oxford Reference Dictionary, 1986, Oxford: Clarendon Press.

Parekh B., 2000, *The Future of Multi-ethnic Britain: The Parekh Report*, Commission on the Future of Multi-ethnic Britain, London: Profile Books.

Park R. E., 1950, *Race and Culture*, New York: Free Press.

Park R. E. and Burgess E. W., 1921, *Introduction to the Science of Sociology*, Chicago: University of Chicago Press.

Parsons T., 1968, *The Structure of Social Action*, New York: Free Press.

Pavkovic A., 1998, From Yugoslavism to Serbism: the Serb national idea 1986–96, *Nations and Nationalism*, 4(4): 511–28.

Ramet S. P., 1996, Nationalism and the 'idiocy' of the countryside: the case of Serbia, *Ethnic and Racial Studies*, 19(1): 70–87.

Rattansi A., 1994, 'Western' racisms, ethnicities and identities in a 'postmodern' frame, in Rattansi A. and Westwood S. (eds), *Racism, Modernity and Identity on the Western Front*, Cambridge: Polity.

Rattansi A., 2002, Racism, sexuality and political economy: Marxism/Foucault/'Postmodernism', in Fenton S. and Bradley H. (eds), *Ethnicity and Economy: 'Race and Class' Revisited*, London: Palgrave, pp. 42–63.

Rex J., 1973, *Race, Colonialism and the City*, London: Routledge and Kegan Paul.

Rex J., 1996, *Ethnic Minorities in the Modern Nation State*, London: Macmillan.

Rex J. and Moore R., 1967, *Race, Community and Conflict*, London: Oxford University Press.

Rex J. and Tomlinson S., 1979, *Colonial Immigrants in a British City: A Class Analysis*, London: Routledge and Kegan Paul.

Roberts R., 1990, *The Classic Slum: Salford Life in the First Quarter of the Century*, Harmondsworth: Viking Penguin.

Robertson R., 1992, *Globalization: Social Theory and Global Culture*, London: Sage.

Rodriguez C., 2000, *Changing Race: Latinos, the Census, and the History of Ethnicity in the United States*, New York: New York University Press.

Rodriguez C. and Cordero-Guzman H., 1992, Placing race in context, *Ethnic and Racial Studies*, 15(4): 523–42.

Samad Y., 1992, Book-burning and race relations: political mobilisation of Bradford Muslims, *New Community*, 18(4): 507–19.

Scott G. M., 1990, A resynthesis of the primordial and circumstantial approaches to ethnic group solidarity: towards an explanatory model, *Ethnic and Racial Studies*, 13(2): 147–71.

Sekulic D., 1997, The creation and dissolution of the multinational state: the case of Yugoslavia, *Nations and Nationalism*, 3(2): 165–80.

Shaw A., 1988, *A Pakistani Community in Britain*, Oxford: Blackwell.

Shils E., 1957, Primordial, personal, sacred and civil ties, *British Journal of Sociology*, 8(2): 130–45.

Simons A., 1997, Democratisation and ethnic conflict: the kin connection, *Nations and Nationalism*, 3(2): 273–90.

Smith A. D., 1981, *The Ethnic Revival in the Modern World*, Cambridge: Cambridge University Press.

Smith A. D., 1986, *The Ethnic Origin of Nations*, Oxford: Blackwell.

Smith S. J., 1989, *The Politics of 'Race' and Residence: Citizenship, Segregation and White Supremacy in Britain*, Cambridge: Polity.

Solomos J., 1993, *Race and Racism in Britain*, London: Macmillan.

Solomos J. and Back L., 1996, *Racism and Society*, London: Macmillan.

Steinberg S., 1981, *The Ethnic Myth: Race, Ethnicity and Class in America*, Boston: Beacon Press.

Steinberg S. (ed.), 2000, *Race and Ethnicity in the United States, Issues and Debates*, Oxford: Blackwell.

Stepanov V., 2000, Ethnic tensions and separatism in Russia, *Journal of Ethnic and Migration Studies*, 26(2), April: 333–55.

Sunday Telegraph, 13 August 1989, Will this be the death of England? (David Lovibond).

Sunday Telegraph, 15 October 2000, We know in our hearts what Britain means (Andrew Roberts).

Taylor C. M., 1994, *Multiculturalism: Examining the Politics of Recognition*, Princeton: Princeton University Press.

Tishkov V., 1997, *Ethnicity, Nationalism and Conflict in and after the Soviet Union: The Mind Aflame*, London: Sage.

Tishkov V., 2000, Forget the nation: post-nationalist understanding of nationalism, *Ethnic and Racial Studies* 23(4): 625–50.

Tönnies F., 1963, *Community and Society*, New York: Harper and Row.

Triandafyllidou A., Calloni M. and Mikrakis A., 1997, New Greek nationalism, <*http://www.socresonline.org.uk/socresonline/ 2/1/7.html*>, *Sociological Research Online*, 2(1).

UNHCR, 2002, UNHCR basic facts, <*http://www.unhcr.ch/cgi-bin/texis/vtx/home?page=basics*>, UNHCR.

US Bureau of the Census, 2000, Racial and ethnic classifications used in Census 2000 and beyond, <*http://www.census.gov/ population/www/socdemo/race/racefactcb.html*>, US Bureau of the Census.

Van Den Berghe P., 1981, *The Ethnic Phenomenon*, New York: Elsevier Press.

Vann Woodward C., 1964, *American Counterpoint*, Boston: Little, Brown.

Virdee S., 1995, *Racial Violence and Harassment*, London: Policy Studies Institute.

Warner W. L. and Srole L., 1945, *The Social Systems of American Ethnic Groups*, New Haven, CT: Yale University Press.

Waters M. C., 1990, *Ethnic Options: Choosing Identities in America*, Berkeley: University of California Press.

Waters M. C., 1999, *Black Identities: West Indian Immigrant Dreams and American Realities*, Cambridge, MA: Harvard University Press.

Weber M., 1978, *Economy and Society*, Berkeley: University of California Press.

Wetherell M. and Potter J., 1992, *Mapping the Language of Racism: Discourse and the Legitimation of Exploitation*, London: Harvester Wheatsheaf.

Wieviorka M., 1994, Racism in Europe: unity and diversity, in Rattansi A. and Westwood S. (eds), *Racism, Modernity and Identity on the Western Front*, Cambridge: Polity, pp. 173–88.

Wieviorka M., 1995, *The Arena of Racism*, London: Sage.

Williams R., 1958, *Culture and Society 1780–1950*, New York: Harper and Row.

Wilson W. J., 1980, *The Declining Significance of Race*, Chicago: University of Chicago Press.

Wilson W. J., 1999, When work disappears: new implications for race and urban poverty in the global economy, *Ethnic and Racial Studies*, 22(3), May: 479–99.

Woo D., 2000, *Glass Ceilings and Asian Americans*, New York: Altamira Press.

Yinger M. J., 1994, *Ethnicity*, New York: State University of New York Press.

Index